Performing for Tourists

Redefining Performances, Performers and Audiences

Performing for Tourists

Redefining Performances, Performers and Audiences

Shiva Rijal

D.K. Printworld (P) Ltd.
New Delhi

Cataloging in Publication Data — DK

[Courtesy: D.K. Agencies (P) Ltd. <docinfo@dkagencies.com>]

Rijal, Shiva, 1973-

Performing for tourists : redefining performances, performers and audiences / Shiva Rijal.

p. cm.

Study on Balinese performance culture practised for the tourists in Ubud, Bali Island, Indonesia.

Includes bibliographical references (p.).

Includes index.

ISBN 13: 9788124605431

ISBN 10: 8124605432

1. Culture and tourism — Indonesia —Ubud. 2. Performing arts — Indonesia — Ubud. 3. Balinese (Indonesian people) — Songs and music. I. Title.

DDC 306.481909598 22

First published in India, 2010

ISBN 13: 978-81-246-0543-1 (Hb) ISBN 10: 81-246-0543-2

Published and printed by:

D.K. Printworld (P) Ltd.

Regd. office : *'Srikunj,'* F-52, Bali Nagar

Ramesh Nagar Metro Station

New Delhi – 110 015

Phones : (011) 2545 3975; 2546 6019; *Fax* : (011) 2546 5926

E-mail: indology@dkprintworld.com

Web: www.dkprintworld.com

For

Abhi Subedi,

a father, guru, and friend

Preface

My involvement in the performance culture studies is only a decade old. I became familiar with the Balinese performance culture as an important topic for research through the works of Clifford Geertz and Richard Schechner for the first time. My interest in it grew further as I started reading and writing on the Newari performance culture of the Kathmandu Valley, Nepal which coincided with my ongoing research on "Cross-Cultural Theatre" for my PhD. This book developed out of this juncture of my career.

The age-old traditional Newar dance and drama forms in the Kathmandu Valley have faced hard times as they are performed only on a few cultural occasions in a year though one cannot deny the fact that a large number of local and metropolitan audience would love to watch them throughout the year. The community-based organizational forms created to manage and look after such art and cultural modes of expressions in the past in the Valley have not been able to spell out their pragmatic roles in the process of continuity and change in the state of the Newar performance culture in the Kathmandu of our times. A culture of disseminating traditional dance and drama forms among the youths of all sexes is yet to be invented though the cultural and tourism policy makers have always harped on traditional performance culture of the Valley to widen the sphere of tourism business in Nepal. Therefore, discourses about traditional Balinese dance and drama forms thriving in the recent times in the context of tourism business made me realize the rationale of conducting the research that this book is mainly based upon.

I set out to research on the Balinese performance culture practised for the tourists in Ubud under the hypothesis that the Asian countries, for that matter, any communities in the world, should live not only with the feeling of sharing a common heritage of arts and cultural practices of the older days but also with the awareness about the reality of the present times when transformations are taking place in the realms of such arts and cultural practices emanating from the cross-cultural movements of the people, especially the tourists.

My encounter with the culture of "performing for tourists" in Ubud (Bali) came as an intervention in my system of understanding the traditional dance, drama and musical forms in the context of globalization. I take this as a source of inspiration and guidance for my further works. But I must say here that I am not a bureaucrat nor am I involved in any governmental body of cultural policy makers. Similary, I am not involved in sectors of cultural tourism as such. I am a theatre person and an academic by profession. Therefore, I feel free to formulate the narrative that this book unfolds.

I take the performance culture practised for the tourists in Ubud as a proof of the fact that traditional dance, drama and musical forms too can draw global and metropolis audience on a regular basis. The "worlders" of the culture of performing for tourists in Ubud live a reality which is that they are not the breachers of the matrix of the cultural and spiritual order that their art forms are often associated with. Neither can they be defined as mere "opportunity and pressure" grabbers and bearers brought in by tourism business. As the custodians of their ages-old art and culture, they have redefined themselves, and their traditional organisational forms set to manage their traditional dance, drama and ceremonies in a new cultural context. They, as the "worlders" of the culture of performing for tourists have created an important zone of dissemination of the art and skills of dance and music of the traditional order in Ubud. A significant number of children, youths and women of all generations and sexes are found engaged in the regular round of learning traditional dance and drama forms in different *sanggars*, which are the learning centres in Ubud. As a result the number of performing groups has increased in the recent times, so has the strength of the semiotics and ideology associated with the traditional Balinese dance and drama forms that have expanded in recent times.

This book is a result of my quest as a theatre person. It is a narration of my personal experience of watching over two thousand artists performing for the tourists in Ubud and around. During my research, I watched over 150 performances made for tourists including the ones carried out as part of the temple ceremonies. My meeting with several writers, researchers and artists from Bali and around the world has helped me to formulate the present narration. Therefore, I must express my gratitude to the performers whom I met in Ubud as well as their audience. I found myself amidst the wonders and epiphanies as I watched the world-famous art practitioners performing on a regular basis for the metropolitan audiences, the tourists. The state of traditional Newar dance and drama forms and their practitioners in the Kathmandu Valley coursed through my mind as I watched the works of the Balinese artists performing for the tourists. I wrote a couple of articles on the possibility of creating a similar performing culture in Kathmandu and got them published in the national dailies. Thus the narrative that this book unfolds has been indirectly set by the socio-aesthetic context of the place that I belong to physically as well as emotionally.

I must state here again, I am neither a bureaucrat nor a cultural policy maker but a theatre person and academician. Moreover, I am very much aware that my stay in Ubud was only a nine-month-long. I am responsible for any discourses demanding lengthier treatments, and errors.

Contents

Acknowledgements

THE Asian Scholarship Foundation (ASF) granted me a nine-month-long scholarship to carry out research in Bali (Indonesia) from October 2006 to July 2007, and a fund to conduct a theatre festival entitled "Culture in Theatre" and a seminar "Redefining Traditional Dance and Drama Forms" in December 2008 in Kathmandu. These supports directly helped me to prepare this book. Similarly, the Social Science Research Council (SSRC) supported my research on the early modern performance culture of the Kathmandu Valley from December 2005 to July 2006, and August – October 2007. Prof. Abhi Subedi, a contemporary Nepali poet and playwright, my *guru*, supervised my PhD dissertation on "Cross-cultural Theatre" from 2000 to 2005. Therefore, I would like to thank them, the institutes and the person for their support and guidance.

I would like to thank Dr Lourdes G. Salvador and the ASF staffs in Bangkok, the Institute Seni Indonesia (ISI) Denpasar, Prof. Dr I. Nyoman Sedana, Prof. I. Wayan Rai, and the ISI Staff, the Central Department of English (Tribhuvan University), Nepal, the Indonesian Institute of Sciences (LIPI) and its staff, especially Dr Ruben Siltunga, the Ford Foundation (Jakarta) and Dr Ujjwal Pradhan, the Indonesian International Education Foundation (IIEF) for helping me get my official documents done in time in Kathmandu, Jakarta and Bali. Prof. Sedana helped me to reach out to several communities of the artists and academicians in Bali. His family also helped me to settle down in Ubud. Dr Pradhan provided me some important research materials.

The seminars and discussion programmes I attended during 2006-09 also have helped me to formulate and foreground the issue that this book is based upon. I thank the organizers of the seminars and discussion programmes mainly the Social Science Research Council, the Asian Scholarship Foundation, the South and South-East Asian Association for the Study of Culture and Religion (SSEARS), and the Kathmandu-based research and academic centres: The Gurukul Theatre School, The Martin Chautari, The Social Science Baha and the Central Department of English.

I thank the following Balinese artists who lead different performing groups and perform for tourists in Ubud: A.A. Anom Putra, Kadek Dewi Aryani, Anak Agung Sri Utari, Anak Agung Raka Astuti, I. Wayan "Lilir" Sujapa, Tjokorda Raka Swastika, Putu Suadini, I. Wayan Danayasa, I. Dewa Putu Rai, I. Made Rajin, I. Ketut Pasek, I. Made Gender, I. Ketut Gde Suarta, Anak Agung Gde Buda Sastra, Anak Agung Gde Bagus Suyoga, Ketut Badra, I. Wayan Warta, I. Wayan Nama, Anak Agung Gde Raka, Desak Nyoman Suarti, Ketut Rupa, Ni Wayan Prilini, I. Wayan Turun, I. Made Sadia, A.A. Gde Oka Dalem, I. Wayan Putih Subadi, I. Ketut Sandi, I. Ketut Suyasa, I. Wayan Jaya Marta, S. Sn, I. Wayan Roja, Tjokorde Alit Hendrawan, Tjok Gde Raka Sukawati, I. Nyoman Martajaya, Ketut Suartana, I.G.A. Raka Rasmi, Tjokorde Alit Dalem, I. Made Sumendra, I. Made Winastra, Nyoman Purfa and I Made Sudarma among others. They were easily available for interviews; without their co-operation, it would not have been possible to accomplish my work in time. Therefore, I would like to appreciate their help to me.

Putu Suadini, my landlady and a local woman artist as well as leader of two groups performing for tourists in Ubud invited me to attend several rituals, ceremonies and performances carried out in her family and the village temples. She allowed me to observe her groups' activities: process of recruiting a new member, managing rehearsal, running social activities, and performing for tourists as well as for temple ceremonies.

A.A. Gede Oka Dalem, Kadek Dewi Aryani, Tjokorde Alit Hendrawan, I.G.A. Raka Rasmi and Tjokorda Raka Swastika helped me to understand some nuances of the Peliatan-based dance and drama forms. Without their support, I would never have been able to trace down the ongoing subtle tussles between the local and the academic forms of Balinese dance and drama in Ubud and Peliatan villages. Meeting with I.G.A. Raka Rasmi, someone trained by the late Mario, the world-famous Balinese dance creator of the twentieth century, helped me to understand the times when several modern Balinese dance and drama forms were practised for the first time in the Peliatan village. I would like to appreciate her sense of aesthetics and humanity.

I would also like to thank I. Made Martanya and Ni Made Sri Harisomawati for assisting my research through teaching me the Bhasa Indonesia. Similarly, I thank Kadek Suardana and Mari of the Arti Foundation, the staffs from the Puri Ubud and the Pondok Pekak Library, painter I. Made Wianta and his wife, the crews of the Nomad Restaurant (Ubud) for their help and hospitality. Ingrid Maurer, a California-based senior installation artist introduced me to several leading painters and expatriates in Bali. Therefore, I would like to thank her and her friends from Ubud for helping me to reach out to some important informants.

Similarly, I thank my senior colleagues and friends Krishna Chandra Sharma, Sangita Rayamajhi, Arun Gupto, Puspa Lal

Damai, Zahed Akter, Santos Das, Deeptha Aachar, Pratyous Onta, Hari Sharma, Manu Manjil, Dhan Bahadur Rokka and Pushpa Acharya for sharing their books and ideas with me. Similarly, I thank Bidur Dangol, my friend and the proprietor of the Vajra Publications for helping me to reach out to the publisher.

Regular email correspondence with my mentor Abhi Subedi, a poet and playwright helped me to nurture my excitement of exploring the performance culture in Ubud. He has always helped me to nourish my dreams and career. To him, I would like to dedicate this book.

My godmother, Bindu Subedi and brothers Salil and Girish Subedi have always remained a source of inspirations to me. I love them very much. Similarly, my brothers Bishnu, Badri, and sisters Madan, Sarala and Dewata have always taken my life and dreams with great love and care. I love and thank them for encouraging me to believe in my dreams.

Finally, I thank my wife, Shraddha for encouraging me to explore the world that I vow to live with freely but honestly.

October 2009
Kathmandu

Shiva Rijal

List of Ilustrations

(Photo credit: Shiva Rijal)

fig. 1. Seen in the picture are local kids learning dances in Sanggar in the Puri Ubud.

fig. 2. Seen in the picture is a nine year-old-girl artist performing for the tourists. She belongs to a group called Nirtta Dewi.

fig. 3. Seen in the picture is a ticket seller waiting for tourists to approach him near the courtyard of the Puri Ubud.

fig. 4. Audiences in most of the venues are welcomed and bid farewell in Japanese as well as English languages.

fig. 5. Seen in the picture is the monument erected in the memory of those killed in the 2002 Bali Bombing in Kuta.

fig. 6 Seen in the picture is a recently formed women's gamelan group from Ubud. I frequently visited the rehearsal that the group went through. After the ritual of mesakapan — the marriage ceremony between the musical instruments and performers, the group is about to stage their creation for the representatives from the LISTIBIYA and local custodians of dance and drama forms.

fig. 7. Seen in the picture is a scene of mesakapan, a ritual performed to mark the marriage between musical instruments and musicians or performers.

fig. 8. Seen in the picture are Tjokorda Ngurah Suyadnya (second from the right), Wakil Legislatif from the Puri Saraswati Ubud, the representative of the LISTIBIYA and the music instructor Swastika Raka (the first from the left)watching the performance of the newly formed women's gamelan.

fig. 9. On the occasions of temple ceremonies, local, tourists and expats gather to watch the same performance that the tourists watch on a regular basis in Ubud.

fig. 10. The scene is from a Mahabharata-based dance drama, where Abhimanyu, the son of Arjuna is fighting a battle known as chakravyuha. All of the performers are in their early teens and belong to a group called Chandra Wirabhuana.

fig. 11. In the recent years, Japanese tourists have become the most visible audience of the performance culture in Ubud.

fig. 12. This dance is known as Chandrawarshi, ISI's creation and is one of the most performed pieces for the tourists in Ubud.

fig. 13. Seen in the picture is a contemporary creation of the group called Nirtta Dewi.

fig. 14. Seen in the picture is Meghanada's magical arrow that has miserably entrapped Rama and Laksmana.

fig. 15. Seen in the picture is a 'naturalistic' dragon used and performed to depict the war between Rawana and Rama by the Cecak group from Jungjugan village.

fig. 16. Seen in the board is the schedule of performances for tourists in Puri Agung in Peliatan.

fig. 17. Seen in the picture is a photo of the late Agung Mandera, the man who played an important role in carving out identity for dance and music in Peliatan style.

fig. 18. Seen in the picture are identity cards of the members of the group. The card contains records of his or her attendance and earning.

fig. 19. In the recent years, ceremonies in Ubud have become more spectacular. Most of the performing groups contribute major part of their income to certain temple as well as to the community funds that are spent for buying paraphernalia that are required for conducting ceremonies.

fig. 20. Seen in the picture is a board mentioning about the schedule for performance put in front of the Banjar building in the Monkey Forest area.

fig. 21. Seen in the picture is Raka Rashmi who was trained by the late Mario. She is in her seventies and teaches dance to children from the local communities in the Arma Museum, Pangosekan.

fig. 22. Seen in the picture are local children learning dances in the Arma Museum. At the far corner is seen Raka Rasmi, someone who was trained by the late Mario, the genius, who is supposed to have given the Kebyar phenomenon a greater magnitude.

fig. 23. A local priest is purifying the venue before the performers appear on the stage.

fig. 24. Seen in the picture is a moment when audiences find themselves intensely watching a performance.

fig. 25. Seen in the picture is the magnificent stage inside the Banjar building at the Monkey Forest Area, and artists performing 'welcome dance' to their audiences, the tourists.

1

Route to Bali

Traditional Dance, Drama and Tourists

TRADITIONAL dance, drama and musical forms and their performances are often taken as "windows" or "socio-aesthetic mirrors" that help one to understand about the culture of people living in a certain geo-cultural and temporal space. They have remained a very important subject of interest for post-colonial researcher and Western anthropologists and theatre creators. Since it is argued that cultures are "most fully expressed" in ritual and theatrical performances (Turner, 1), by observing traditional dance, drama and rituals and their structures including the time and the context that they are performed at, he or she can know about the lives of the people at both the tangible and intangible levels. However, traditional dance, drama and musical forms can also be the subject of aesthetic and metaphysical contemplation of their practitioners and custodians. Therefore, much also depends on how practitioners or the "artworlders" of the traditional dance and drama forms do define their art forms, culture and profession. The following remarks made by Sanjukta Panigrahi, a world renowned Odissi dancer, regarding her experience of carving out professionalism in her career reveals that transformation in traditional dance and drama forms emanates from the "critical" concentration that an individual practitioner makes on the very medium of art:

> I paid great attention to technique, but I felt a certain emptiness inside me. I went to my master: "I am too dominated by technique. I want to work in a way which combines technique and emotion, creating new images." My master replied: "Put drama into your dance. Do it through silent dialogue, otherwise you will not be able to express yourself. You must have both technique and feelings." I began to rehearse different dialogues based on the same phrases, and so obtained new images. "You must dominate the technique," said my master, "and be capable of ignoring it." (Panigrahi, 89)

Since the traditional dance and drama forms are performed for certain deities, by certain families of performers, on certain dates and in certain venues within a certain community sphere, they survive in a limited zone of practice and patterns of dissemination. But by their very "generic" nature, traditional dance and drama forms can thrive and survive only when they are practised on a regular basis. Performers and audiences need to meet on a regular basis to create a wider sphere of dissemination and practice, and enhance a secure future for such art forms. The greater the number of practitioners and learners, the richer remains the heritage of traditional dance and drama forms. Moreover, only regular meetings between and among professionals, amateurs, learners of all ages and sexes on the one hand, and audience on the other hand, can enable the stakeholders to create a vibrant zone for traditional dance and drama forms' survival and expansion.

Tourists as audience in Bali, especially in Ubud, have stimulated the practitioners of the traditional dance and drama forms, and locals of all generations and sexes as well as university graduates involve into rigorous rehearsals to make the traditional performance culture function on a regular basis. This culture of performing for the tourists in Ubud has eased the great flow of skills and crafts of the practitioners of the very traditional dance, drama and music. More importantly, it has also intensified the very culture of forming and managing groups not only with the purpose of performing for the tourists but also for giving continuity for the community activities such as the temple ceremonies, rituals and festivals in spectacularly vibrant forms. The researchers on the Balinese performance culture of the present times as well as the local art practitioners, discussed in the following chapters, believe that the traditional dances and dramas in Ubud have thrived in the recent years because of the tourism business. This has also given to the Ubudians an important hope that the traditional dance and musical forms like modern theatre, paintings and literature too can flourish here in various styles and thematic forms.

Moreover, this culture of performing dance, drama and musical forms of various origins and natures for tourists in Ubud has given rise to a creative tension among the local artists themselves as they work with a kind of meta-consciousness for the tourists. Deep down, they realize that they should not keep on practising the same art form for tourists for a long time. Therefore, they have developed a system of cross-checking each other's works. They also argue about the homogeneity "created" by academy in the Balinese dance and drama forms, and speak about the importance of introducing and maintaining variations in them. The many senior artists I came across criticised the current trends of academicizing the traditional Balinese dance and musical forms by freezing them in a specific form of choreography and notation system. They argue that promotion of any dance and musical form in a monolithic style, no matter how perfect it may be, can threaten the very heritage of diversity from within. The greater the variations, the more vibrant remain the individual dance and musical forms. The Balinese artists in Ubud practise this very reality. They are worried about their children for not being genuinely interested to learn and perform their own traditional art forms. Therefore, they are actively involved in creating forums, known as *sanggar* so that their children can learn and practise the traditional dance, drama and musical forms on a regular basis (see *fig.* 1). Importantly, such forums are managed from a community fund that is created by the donations of some part of their income as a matter of rule by the groups performing for the tourists. The leaders of the village organization as well as the performing groups in Ubud seem very concerned about supporting the local children, youths and women from their communities to form what they call "gamelan" groups and develop professionalism in their dance, drama and musical forms (see *fig.* 2).

There are over forty groups which perform for tourists in Ubud on a regular basis. They work with the agents of tourism business such as the travel agencies, hoteliers and ticket-sellers to create a greater flow of tourists, who comprise the audience to their venues, and, in the meantime, they are intensely engaged in rehearsing dance, drama and music on distinct themes and styles. This makes one to realize a fact that the culture of performing for tourists in Ubud is performing the culture of a serious and pragmatic nature; not a mere exercise done for the sake of earning easy money but a wiser act of expanding the very sphere by disseminating the art and craft of traditional dance and drama forms through the medium of regular performances. It is this very theme that this book is based on.

Framework

In the remaining part of this chapter, I locate my position as a researcher, and introduce the cultural and the academic background that I come from. Therefore, readers will find a brief introduction to the Newar performance culture of the

Kathmandu Valley, followed by another brief introduction to the intercultural theatre, the subject of my doctorate research, in the second half of this chapter. The next chapter makes a brief survey of the researches made on the Balinese performance culture. Along with my personal experience of carrying out research in Ubud, I argue that the locals, researchers and tourists have played very important roles in promoting not only tourism business but also the very traditional performing arts and cultures in Bali. I then argue that the culture of performing for tourists in Bali, especially in Ubud, functions with multiple voices and visions, thrills and limitations which is the subject of the third chapter of this book. The culture of performing for tourists and aesthetics associated with it need to be taken as part of the history and aesthetics of the Balinese performing arts. By performing for the tourists, the Balinese art practitioners have broadened the very domain of their art forms — the subject of the fourth chapter of this book. In the fifth chapter, I argue that the culture of performing for tourists on a regular basis has helped the Balinese in Ubud to practise and learn the art, skill and wisdom of training children, youth and female artists and work in a network in a newer context brought in by tourism. Tourists as regular audience of the traditional Balinese dance and drama forms have made one to redraw the boundaries between and among the locals, researchers, expatriates, business makers and tourists in Bali which is the subject of the sixth chapter. In the last chapter, I briefly discuss about the exigency of performing traditional dance and drama forms on a regular basis, and draw parallels with the Newar performance culture of the Kathmandu Valley.

Research Route to Bali

The nature and scope of this work is strongly set by the performance culture of the Kathmandu Valley where I have lived for two decades. Researchers on the art and culture of the Valley have defined the Newar performance culture as "cosmogonic" where gods, demons and humans coexist. Dance and drama performances and cultural processions in the Valley are taken as an act of communication with gods. "The Valley dwellers believe in gods and feel that the gods reciprocate through their engagement with the human world. Festivals in the towns of Kathmandu Valley are a fascinating depiction of this romantic perspective. Residents play-act and animate gods as if their great-grandfathers had seen them walking the streets only a few decades ago" (2002: 10), writes Sudarshan Raj Tiwari, a well-known Nepali architect and researcher on the Valley's performance culture. Evoking the natural bond between gods and human beings that the Newars celebrate though their rituals and festivals, Tiwari further argues, "gods in the Valley are supposed to come out from their temples and renew their relations with humans, just as humans, as believers, visit the gods in their temples. Either way, for the residents of Kathmandu, the result is joy and festivals" (2002: 9).

Similarly, the performance culture in the Valley is supposed to have taken such a strong root that "the urban space of Newar town is essentially a ritual space. The streets, the squares form the setting for a variety of ritual performances which are bound to the festival calendar of the year" (1980: 57), writes Jan Pieper, a European researcher on South Asian performance culture. This nature of performance culture is also reflected in the traditional architecture of the Valley that cannot be "rigorously categorized as sacred or secular, for all serve both gods and men. The common houses and royal palaces alike have private chapels, shrines, and special places for worship" (1998: 128), writes Mary Slusser, an American scholar on Newar art and culture of the Valley. And, this sharing of space between gods and human beings is "the major theatrical spirit of the people" and the main spirit behind "performance arts in Nepal Mandala" (2006: 24), writes Abhi Subedi, a contemporary Nepali playwright. And, the Newar farmers in the Valley are credited for maintaining this very heritage of the performance culture of the Valley. They since millennia have blended folk tunes with classical "by creating accessible and flexible rhythms for singing and performance, and developed one's own forms" (1989: 11), writes Jagadish Rana, a senior Nepali scholar on Newar performance culture. This academic awareness about the Newar performance culture of the Valley helped me to set up the basis of rationale of carrying out research on the Balinese traditional performance culture practised for tourists. However, this book is not a comparative study between these two performance cultures.

Cross-cultural Theatre and Beyond

Traditional dance and drama forms have also been taken as the subjects and sources that can give a new lease of life to the modern, post-modern and post-colonial theatres in the West and the East. But it is important to realize that they too can be performed as they "are" in their plural forms. Peter Brook, Eugenio Barba, Richard Schechner and Ariane Mnouchkine among other intercultural theatre creators of the West have worked with the practitioners of the traditional dance and drama from the non-Western societies, and have carried out cross-cultural experimentations in their theatres. They have defined their intercultural experimentations as a methodology or process of learning each other's cultural modes of expression and bringing new awareness in the post-modern theatrics of the West. Such experimentations have revealed to them that the *modus operandi* of the Western realistic theatrics has brought limitation in the very imaginative spirit of theatre art. This awareness or meta-theatrical consciousness has created departures from the mainstream Western theatre. Traditional dance and drama forms of different parts of the world have inspired the Western theatre creators and thinkers to revitalize their theatre forms and discourses. Eugenio Barba, a European cross-cultural theatre practitioner writes,

> For a spectator from the West, there is nothing more suggestive than a traditional Asian performance seen in its context, often in the open tropical air, with a large and reactive audience, with a constant musical accompaniment which captivates the nervous system, with sumptuous which delight the eye, and performers who embody the unity of actor-dancer-singer-storyteller. (1994: 05)

Such spirit of traditional dance and drama forms has not only delighted the Western audience like Barba but has also given them a new sense of theatre aesthetics that a cross-cultural understanding in theatre, performance culture for that matter, can open up new perspectives (Victor Turner 1982: 18).

Western intercultural theatre creators or experimenters are large in numbers. Ralph Yarrow, a European critic on Indian theatre calls such theatre researchers and experimenters the "travellers" (2001: 33-34). Intercultural theatre creators from the West have visited several local cultural sites and worked with the performers belonging to different cultural and art communities. As a result, they have tested one kind of performance techniques with the other and drawn knowledge and wisdom of theatre making skills, crafts and techniques from such comparisons. Patrice Pavis, a critic on intercultural theatre writes that interculturality in the theatre of our times should be taken as "a crucible in which performance techniques are tested against and amalgamated with the techniques that receive and fashion them" (1996: 2). For example, by producing *Richard II* of Shakespeare in the Japanese Kabuki style, Ariane Mnouchkine tried neither to revitalize the Japanese indigenous forms of performance arts nor did she try to adapt Shakespeare to the codes of *Noh, Kabuki* or *Bunraku* performance arts (Godrad 1999: 92) but made an attempt of extending the very nature and nuances of modern theatrics of the West. Similarly, traditional dances and dramas have been used as part of exploring the alternative mode of looking at theatre art and life in the post-colonial context. Girish Karnad, a contemporary Indian playwright writes that the energy of folk theatres enables one to make, "the simultaneous presentation of alternative points of view, of alternative attitudes to the central problem" (2000: 14). Thus it is argued and believed that folk or traditional forms of theatrical practices are not mere semiotic forms only. They can neither be taken as the rudimentary of cultures.

But traditional dance and drama forms practised for tourists in Ubud in Bali have revealed to us their important strength other than noticed by anthropologists and theatre creators. Balinese dances were performed in the *Colonial Exposition* in 1931 in Paris, for that matter, in the West for the first time, and were watched by Antonine Artaud, one of the pioneers of the cross-cultural experimentation in theatre of the West. Artaud is credited for bringing some ground breaking theories and experimentations in the European theatre of his time. But the traditional Balinese dance, drama and musical forms that Artaud and his colleagues and disciples had watched and have worked on have revealed another important fact that they too can be performed as they "are," in their plural forms, not necessarily as a source of experimentation for modern, post-modern and post-colonial theatrics of the present times. This must be taken as an important achievement made by the Balinese dancers and musicians.

In the course of my nine-month-long stay in Ubud, I watched over 120 performances made for tourists, and over three dozen performances made on several cultural occasions. During the period, I encountered a performing group going through a regular round of rehearsal to meet official "standardness." I also watched groups, one formed out of mainly university graduates, and the other of women performers from different communities, making their debut performances. Some old groups revised some of their dance and drama forms as they had to recruit new members in their teams. This study and experience of mine in Ubud has revealed to me that the performance culture practised in Ubud can also be taken as the source of inspiration across great many cultural communities in Asia and elsewhere.

Limitations

This book is about the culture of performing traditional dance, drama and musical forms for tourists, and is based on the research conducted in Ubud (Bali, Indonesia). As a discourse made on traditional dance and drama forms practised for tourists in Ubud, this book is conditioned by the socio-cultural background that I come from, on the one hand, and the research works made by the scholars from the West and Bali (Indonesia) on Balinese performance culture, on the other. In this plethora of cross-cultural interpretation of the Balinese performance culture, the locals in Ubud are working in a uniquely cross-cultural atmosphere, but while doing it, the Ubudians perform their art, skill and wisdom of managing the heritage of Balinese dance and musical forms in a pragmatic manner.

Readers looking for a history and aesthetics of any individual Balinese dance and drama form in detail may not find this book of any help. Similarly, readers who are looking for a comprehensive history and theories on the Balinese performing arts also may not find this book helpful. This book also does not provide any empirical data and information on the Balinese art industry in the context of tourism business. This book is the quest of a researcher who is interested in creating the culture of practising traditional dance, drama and music on a regular basis. I argue that like the modern forms of art such as literature, music, theatre and paintings among the others, traditional dance and drama forms too can have its audience on a regular basis and can achieve the transformations through constant contemplation on and experimentation of their performers.

This book is based on the research carried out in Ubud: Ubud, Peliatan, Pedang Tangal, Buntuyun and Junjugan communities. Therefore, Ubud as a collective noun stands as a place different from Kuta, Sanur and Nusa Dua, the other touristic places in Bali, whereas Ubud as a particular village is different from Peliatan, Padang Tangal, Buntuyun and Junjugan.

Finally, performing a research work on the culture of performing for tourists in Ubud, as far as my experience goes, is determined by the corpus of research works already performed on Bali's art and culture by the Balinese as well as non-Balinese researchers, the recent social transformations of which the Balinese themselves are the agents, the opinions that the Balinese performers in Ubud across all ages and genders put forward, and of course, the personal concerns and impressions of the researcher which is the subject of the next chapter.

2

Tourists, Researchers and the Ubudian Performance Culture

Tourists as Audience

IT is 7 o'clock in the evening in Ubud. Tourists start to pop in and around the venues where the Balinese dance, drama and musical forms are staged for them on a regular basis. The ticket-sellers (see *fig.* 3) stand in every corner of the street and do not let even a single tourist pass unnoticed. With tickets in their hands, tourists enter the venue and start occupying their seats and wait for the performance to begin in a calm mood. Tourists make up an amorphous and the ever shifting audience of the traditional, modern and contemporary Balinese dance, drama and musical forms in Ubud. This amorphous audience is thought to have replaced the former patrons and audience of feudal kings and lords, who catered to their own tastes by making their subjects, the common folks to perform for them. But, no matter how amorphous the tourists/ audiences may remain, they have left certain traces of interest and preferences in Ubud's performance culture. If tourists stay at places far from Ubud and come here with a purpose of watching performances, they are told or taken to a particular venue by their guides or travel agents. The agents get paid some amount of money in the form of a commission for bringing tourists to their venues. And, if tourists come and stay in Ubud for a couple of days, they become comparatively more informed audience as they select venue, and finally become audience of a heterogeneous structure. But this heterogeneous group of audience in Ubud is linguistically divided into two: English and Japanese. Many performing groups have their brochures printed in both languages, and audiences are welcomed and accorded farewell accordingly (see *fig.* 4).

The audiences (linguistically divided into two) within a couple of days fly back to their home leaving some impacts on the performance culture of Ubud. Performing groups in Ubud hold a view that their audiences prefer some dance and drama forms more than the others. They know that audiences who keep on coming with a gap of certain years want to watch the same dance and drama which they had watched on their last visit. Moreover, groups which have performed abroad also assume that their audiences have specific nationality. Most of the established performing groups in Ubud have performed in Japan and believe that their main audience remains the Japanese, and so they behave accordingly. Tourists as audience too exhibit certain obvious behaviours as they mostly prefer to watch traditional or classical Balinese dance and drama forms. This has made most of the performing groups in Ubud present three traditional, three modern and three contemporary dance and musical creations to their audience. Recently formed groups also follow the same methodology of selecting and combining the "unit" of performances for the tourists, their audience. Groups which have been performing for tourists for over two decades too do not want to replace some of the traditional Balinese dance and drama forms as they are loved by tourists and the locals alike.

Performance culture in Ubud is in a state of continuity and change as the leaders of several performing groups told the researcher that the number of their audience has decreased by 75 per cent to 50 per cent since the 2002 Bali Bombings though the numbers of performing groups have increased in the recent years. Moreover, Japan has become the most tourist-sending-nation to Bali, for that matter to Ubud too. This change in audience structure has brought some diversity into the performance culture of Ubud as the *Bamboo Gamelan*, a popular musical form in Negara, the North Bali, has been recently introduced into Ubud as an attempt to address the interest of the Japanese audience. This act of popularizing the *Bamboo Gamelan* in Ubud was accomplished under the leadership of a Japanese entrepreneur named Suzuki San (Gede Surrya Suzuki), who runs hotel business in Ubud.

Glocal Ubud

Local boundary is "a membrane than a wall" and "leaky, contingent construction" where "global forces are taken up, struggled over, and refracted for site-specific purposes" (Conquergood 2008: 369), and is "no longer endowed with the relative autonomy" (Jameson 2002: 346). Particularly in the context of tourism culture, a local site is often given a shape of a destination "ready for a particular sort of reception and particular tourist practices" (Crang 2004: 78) not by locals alone as so much also depends on "elite and metropolitan efforts" involved "to appropriate and transvalue local traditions and significations" (Appadurai and Breckenridge (1986: 6) in Wiener 1999: 51-52). Several factors make us support a view that Ubud is such a glocal boundary, "a tourist boom-town in a tourism boom-island where people, ideas, and money fresh off aircraft and electronic media from all over the world rub shoulders with each other" (MacRae 1999: 124). It is argued that the researchers, the agents of tourism business and the local elites in the second and the third decades of the last century shared a common vision to create Ubud as artist's colony "where aesthetics and culture would supersede crude materialism" and Ubud, they dreamed as "a Far East version of Monte Verita or Worpswede — a painter's village in the German lowlands" (Reisner 2004: 138). Michel Picard, a French researcher on the Balinese performance culture takes Ubud as a prime example of a place initially distinguished by the Western fantasies, and after Ubud managed to bring more life into its local customs and ceremonies it became "a model resort area, constantly cited as an example of tourism development harmoniously integrated into village life" (1996: 89).

Not only tourism; even terrorism is supposed to have made Bali a glocal space. The 2002 Bali Bombings, the event that is often taken as a consequence of the global political disorder, are thought to have intensified "the daily life of ritual" in Ubud as offerings to the gods have become higher, and the lines of women carrying offerings seemed to be longer, and their concentration seemed to be more intense" (Murdoch 2004: 102). The interviews taken with the local entrepreneurs and the custodians of the performance culture in Ubud confirm that the Ubudians are more interested in and dedicated to 'otherifying' Ubud from other touristic places which are mostly famous for the night life culture in Bali. Since tourists come and stay in Ubud to watch ceremonies and traditional dance and drama forms, the locals in Ubud think that the more they can intensify their rituals, dance and drama performances the greater would be the number of tourists in Ubud bringing greater prosperity to their business as well.

Similarly, expatriates also make Ubud "leaky" as it is taken as "expats' friendly place." Out of 47,000 expatriates in Bali, 8,400 of them live in Ubud. American expats prefer the south side of Ubud; the French and Italians in Sayan, north to Ubud; Swiss, German, Australian and partly Welsh and English live in North Ubud; Danish colony lies somewhere in mid-Ubud (Resiner 2004: 145). Moreover, activities of a group of foreign women — usually the Americans and the Australians married to Balinese men — have established thriving businesses (Murdoch 2004: 105). The world famous phenomenon "the Ubud Reader and Writer Festival" that has started to take place since 2006 annually is a brainchild of an Australian female intellectual Janet married to a Balinese man Ketut. An expat Resiner writes, "For expatriates (and one might find this a bit colonialist in thinking) living here is very often a situation of us and them" (2004: 150).

As Ubud is becoming "leaky," myths and mysteries associated with it are also becoming prominent among the expats and the tourists. Balinger himself an expat in Ubud narrates that a *celuluk* mask was given to a Western couple back in the 1960s as a wedding gift that travelled around the world with them, bringing nightmares to those in close proximity and finally it has come to rest in *Puri* Saren lurking in front of *Puri* to protect the people of Ubud (2004: 26). Ṛṣi Mārkaṇḍeya, a Hindu sage who is supposed to have established the culture and human settlements in Bali, is no longer a local and mythical character of its mysterious past but has become a name and a trope of the spiritual power and authority that expats in Ubud too want to be equipped with.

The *Puri* or palace has remained an important agency in the state of continuity and change of the performance culture in Ubud, thus making Ubud more "leaky." Researchers argue that the *Puri* has managed to play a very safe role to maintain most of its power and wealth, and has developed a tight network of alliances and patronages (Picard 1996: 84, Vickers 1989: 140) in every major political upheaval that has taken place in Bali, for that matter, in the Republic of Indonesia. Howe writes that the Suharto regime (1966-98) helped, whether intentionally or not, to maintain the gentry's influence over the Balinese affairs: "The governors of Bali and the heads of its eight regencies were almost entirely high-caste individuals during these years, a period which has seen the gentry active and successful in local government and in business and commerce" (2001: 82-3). The *Puri* Ubud has initiated many social, economic and cultural activities as it started the first local hotels and established links with travel agencies in Australia (MacRae 1999: 138). It has also maintained the temples and other sacred objects, dance troupes and music ensembles not only in Ubud but also in the villages situated in the very cultural and spiritual routes through which the religion and culture in Bali passed through in the past. Therefore, the *Puri* is often credited for recreating "moral authority" and "a Negara (state) of hearts and minds supported, on the one hand, by material patronage and, on the other, by reactivation of traditional beliefs in divine legitimacy" (MacRae 1999: 143).

Cokorada Gede Raka Sukawati of the *Puri*, though he did not take much care of local artists, as one of the *Puri* members denied to marry the daughter of Lampard, the genius and trend setter in modern Balinese painting (Vickers 1989: 141-42), had played an instrumental role in bringing some historically important artists from the West to Ubud in the period between the Wars. By inviting Walter Spies to live, it is argued that Cokorada Raka was already doing a thing of an important order for making Ubud and its performance culture reach out to the world outside. The *Puri* now presides over or chairs the foundation, *Bina Wisata* established in 1982 to encourage the Ubudians to intensify their cultures to draw tourists and define or give Ubud the shape of a tourist destination. As a result, Ubud now has earned a glocal identity as it won the title "the Best Village of Bali." Moreover, the *Puri* has made an important effort to promote the performance culture in Ubud by providing its courtyard for groups to perform for tourists throughout the week. It also offers its space for the local children and youths to learn and practise traditional dance and musical forms on a regular basis.

Balinese Performance Culture: Continuity and Change

The repertoire of discourses made over a period of several hundred years is a proof that the Balinese performance culture too is a subject of continuity and change. The agents of colonizers, missionaries, tourists, researchers across time and space and the Balinese themselves have felt a need to define or redefine the Balinese performance culture. So much has also depended on the way Indonesia as a modern nation state has defined its art and culture by promulgating cultural and tourism policies. The West, for that matter the travellers from the West to Bali, in the course of 300 years, has "constructed a complex and gorgeous image of the island that has come to take over even Balinese thought" (1989: 2) writes Adrian Vickers. Travellers, agents of tourism business and researchers have happily harped on the exotic images of Bali so much that their discourses have "produced an inward-looking gaze that has blinded observers to broad critical and comparative perspectives" (Rubinston and Connor, 1999: 1). Bali has always fascinated scholars around the world, so much so that as many as one hundred researchers work on Bali a year, and as a result Bali has developed "its own academics" (Vickers 1989: 189) formed of "Balinese views" represented or reported "by non-Balinese writers" (Vickers, 1994: xiii). Thus the researchers on Bali form an ever increasing global community of image creators and interpreters of the Balinese art and culture. This culture of intellectual exercise on Bali has created a wonder as arts and culture of Bali now have been "framed in foreign concepts, and the effect is often bewildering, even to the Balinese themselves" (Picard 1996: 17).

Geoffrey Robinson argues that most of the discourses made by colonial agents and many anthropologists on places like Bali assume a view that "cultural" people could not at the same time be a "political" one (1998: 6). But Balinese in the course of their history have proved that they like people everywhere know-how to "identify with cultural groups: tribes, ethnic groups, religious communities, nations, and at the broadest level, civilizations" and "use politics not just to advance their interests but also to define their identity" (Huntington 1996: 21). They too live a reality that to be human is to "move forward into the future, constantly dragging the chain that binds one to the past" (Valeri 1990: 189), have spoken "from changing roles, in new ways, on behalf of tradition and place" and lived through a reality that "senses of locale are expressed and felt through continuously renegotiated insides and outsides" (Clifford 2001: 16). In this sense, the Balinese can be taken as the most actively involved subjects in the process of taking up global forces to enhance local cultural identity.

Bali's performance culture has always been changing though it is difficult to put "one's finger exactly on the point at which things stopped being what they were and became instead something else" (Geertz 1980: 5) by the time agents of colonizers, missionaries, travellers and researchers started to create discourses on it. Change in Balinese culture is a natural phenomenon, and it "is being caused by the Balinese and those Indonesians living in Bali — a change, quite normal in today's materialistic thinking, which is not only our own, but also the romanticizing view of local intellectuals who often do not want to admit it" (Wilpert 2001: 7). Tourism has heralded a consciousness among Balinese that their performance culture and arts alone can secure a prosperous future for Bali. It has stimulated them to be more active in the act of intensifying their performance culture as a result of which it is believed that despite "predictions by social observers that Bali would become "de-cultured" under the influence of mass tourism, mass media, and the modern capitalist system, a discourse of "Balinese culture" is in fact becoming more potent than ever before. Some signs of this are easy to be located and to be read, for they fit with our assumptions about what culture should be" (Santikarma 2001: 28). For this very reason, the Balinese are praised for possessing "a particular genius in the course of their history for assimilating outside influences in a selective way, adopting only those that suit them, and integrating them harmoniously into their own cultural fabric" (Picard 1996: 11).

Images Bombed

The Bombings that took place on 12 October 2002 in pubs in Kuta (Bali) are supposed to have brought intervention into the "paradise" image of Bali. These horrendous events that took the lives of 202 people and injured 200 more have given rise to multiple discourses which aim to deconstruct the earlier images of the Bali and its cultures (see *fig.* 5). It is taken as a gruesome event that happened one year, one month and one day after the World Trade Centre attack (Couteau 2003: 36). Couteau further writes that this event did not only kill tourists, but also destroyed "the image of the island as "Paradise Bali" and haven of peace in the troubled archipelago. It also precipitated for Bali an unprecedented economic crisis. The spectre of political and economic violence is now looming" (2003: 36). And, this tragic event is thought to have revealed that Bali as "a land of dreams is indeed a myth that has fooled many" (Dwikora 2003: 43).

Moreover, the Bombings are supposed to have created a demarcation line in Bali's cultural history into two: prior and after the bomb. Prior to the Bombings, the Balinese believed that "a magical aura surrounded the island, an aura of strong spiritual power, and that this was so because of the devotion with which its inhabitants performed daily rites meant to ward off evil by appeasing spirits both high and low," but after the bomb "they discovered that 'Bali is safe' was just a myth" (Dwikora 2003: 44). Before the zero hour of 12 October 2002, Bali was sold "as a 'paradise' by international tourism industry and Indonesian marketers of culture, with pictures which were alike throughout decades," and Balinese culture for the tourism business and its agents was "neither the hard work in the rice field, nor the role of women in a patriarchal society" but "rather event like swinging hips of *Legong* dancers, the magic atmosphere of temple feats, the nagging witches and demons, and the lavish death culture with their spectacular cremations" (2003: 56) writes, Urs Ramseyer.

Similarly, the Bombings have evoked other historical and political events of Bali of the past such as the *Perang Puputan* of 1906 when thousands of Balinese both kings and their subjects performed a mass sacrifice in a historical fight against the Dutch Empire, the political unrest of 1965-66 when over a hundred thousand Balinese lost their lives, and the October 1999 mass uprising when the unhappy crowd, the supporters of Sukarnoputri, the former President of Indonesia set fire to the government buildings in Singaraja, Negara and Denpasar causing billions of Rupiah's worth of damage. Balinese too are violent, therefore, it is "inappropriate to portray Bali as a heavenly island, where the people only dance and smile and have never known anger" (Dwikora 2003: 48).

Since the Bombings took place in pubs in Kuta, the most touristic place in Bali, it is taken as a blow "against the West's neo-colonial claims to power and the neo-liberal globalization of economy and culture pushed on people by the USA" and the Indonesian administration under Megawati Sukarnoputri "who got involved in the American war against terrorism" (Ramseyer 2003: 56). It is also taken as an "encounter of two worlds or cultures with their totally different basic attitudes and values. On the one hand, there is the international capital world, which is fought with the language of bombs, and on the other hand there is the Hindu-agrarian world of the Balinese, which protects itself with the language of its symbols, which manifested themselves in a huge ritual, based on the faith of all Hindu-Balinese in *Karmaphala*" (Made Wianta with Ramseyer 2003: 62). Finally, the Bombing is also taken as an event that has taken the curtain off tourism in Bali as the statistical data shows that 70 per cent of all tourism activities are being controlled by the non-Balinese Indonesians and foreigners, and only 14 out of 114 star-awarded hotels are managed by Balinese (Ramseyer 2003: 59).

Performing for Gods and Tourists

Researchers and travellers on and to Bali have highlighted the spiritual aspects of the Balinese dance, drama and musical forms. The culture of performing such Balinese art forms for the tourists that has come to function and flourish since the 1920s is often criticized for creating disruption in the symbiotic relationship between the religion and the performance culture that the Balinese have lived with for ages. It is philosophized that the Balinese dance and theatre tell "the communities between the living and the dead, the visible (*sekala*) and the invisible (*niskala*)" and also reflect "harmony between the small world of humans (*bhawana alit* or microcosms) and the larger world of the universe (*bhawana agung* or macrocosms)" (Couteau 1998: 8-10). The gods in Bali are thought to "enjoy intelligible delights, architecture, and music, dancing, offerings of flowers and fruit; those incredibly beautiful offerings made out of the simplest elements into the utmost elaboration" (Zoete and Spies 1986: 4). Dance and drama in Bali are called appropriately "the work of gods" (Meads 1970: 208). Since the Balinese dance, music and drama are parts of the offerings made to gods, they hold spiritual values of a greater importance. Every cultural occasion in Bali demands the performance of one or the other kinds of dance and drama to be arranged, and one does not need to go to "a specific place to experience art. It happens where a social or religious activity is happening" (Herbest 1997: 114).

But there are a couple of problematics here. First, all art forms are spiritual (Sorell 1967: 17). It is often believed or philosophized that "with the principle in mind that "what delights gods, must delight man" dance was received from the gods as their great gift to man" (Sorell 1967: 52). Second, performances made on religious ceremonies in Bali are activities in which more than "one billion dollars a year" is spent, and "the human labour expended in the ceremonies is in millions of hours a year" (Tisna 2001: 21-22). Therefore, they can be taken as economic burden for Balinese commoners. Tisna further argues that a temple ceremony in Bali is far more than a mere worshipping of God, demigods and ancestors but proclaiming one's prestige, existence, and rank. Third, tourism, which is often taken as secular and thus opposite entity to spiritualism, has played an important role in making ceremonies from *Galungan* to cremation in Bali more spectacular, and has encouraged locals to intensify their rituals and ceremonies further. A variety of traditional dance, drama, music and puppet theatre are offered to gods in every ceremony. Those who perform for gods also perform for tourists, and many performances made for gods are watched by tourists as well. Fourth, performance culture too is a domain of invention and intervention both from within as well as outside as Turner argues that the community and its individual members, who regard themselves "as the masters or 'owners' of ritual and liturgy, or as representatives of the ancestors and gods who ultimately 'own' them, have authority to introduce, under certain culturally determined conditions, elements of novelty from time to time into socially inherited deposit of ritual customs" (1982: 31).

Therefore, spirituality associated with art and culture too is a matter of continuity and change. Dance, drama and musical forms in Bali have defied the very paradigm of categorizing them into spiritual, thus sacred and secular. Tenzer writes that many sacred Balinese music compositions have found their way into secular life, and this has not necessarily lessened the music's ritual power (1991: 76). A *Barong* dance that was created with the purpose of staging it for tourists for the *Hotel Bali*, and *Janger*, an entertaining, secular dance drama prepared with the same purpose, both are performed on temple ceremonies these days. Many dance and musical forms created by academics in Bali too are offered to gods. Leaders of several *Kecak* groups told the researchers that they have performed the same *Kecak* that they perform for tourists for temple ceremonies as well.

Economy of Performing for Tourists

The culture of performing for tourists needs to be taken as part of a larger performance culture that the Balinese have lived with for ages. *Kecak* groups from Sambahan, Taman Kaja, Junjungan and Padang Tegal belong to *banjar*, village community. They donate the money that they make by performing for tourists to a certain community fund created with the purpose of maintaining temple and conducting ceremonies which keep on falling round the year. Since it is obligatory that every house from the *banjar* must contribute some money for conducting ceremonies successfully, groups formed out of the *banjar* members with the purpose of performing for tourists have eased the economic burden for the individual householder. The money earned or collected in the fund is spent for buying fruits, bamboo, cakes and ritualistic paraphernalia that are a must to conduct ceremonies. Groups performing for tourists in temple yard pay mostly 10 per cent of their income to the temple fund. This money is mainly used for maintaining instruments and conducting temple ceremonies. Most of the groups divide money among their members on the day of *galungan* that falls twice a year. The *galungan* days herald inside temple precinct some paraphernalia of offerings such as:

> Golden-flowered aureoles towering above, rice-cakes of various colours and shapes, thin round wafers white and brown, neat packets wrapped in palm-leaf, or the dried, snow-white, compressed grains; sweetmeats twisted like sugar-candy, pink-patterned disks, bananas green and yellow, durians, cucumbers, limes, all hung with palm-leaf stoles of varied design, and surmounted by raying crests of marigold, like branching candlesticks, roast chickens, a frozen fountain, higher than a man made out of the fat of a pig, the inside of his stomach shaped and draped in minute transparent hangings, banners, and umbrellas of filmy lace, the curious cold fabric brightened by touches of scarlet and green pepper pods. (Zoete and Spies, 1986: 4)

Such ritual paraphernalia observed and narrated by Zoete and Spies above in the first half of the twentieth century has become larger these days as several senior locals and the researchers on Balinese culture and tourism often claim. Since groups performing for tourists contribute a significant amount of money to the temple and community fund to run ceremonies, the rituals, performance and ceremonies in Ubud have gone through some phenomenal transformations.

Performers can draw a small amount of money anytime they need it. Dancers who come from next village or other *banjar* are paid on a daily basis. Similarly, government tax officers arrive just in time to check the number of audience at some popular venues especially where groups manage to earn a significant amount of money. Many successful groups, especially those eight performing in *Puri* Ubud pay 10 per cent of their income as tax to the government. Leaders of several groups tell that there is "no hard and fast rule" for paying tax to the government as government officials do not bother to come and take tax from groups that are run by *banjar*. Some recently formed groups do not have to pay for temple fund either. But if they get over 20 guests or audiences, they pay some 2,50,000 Rupiah or 10 per cent of their income as a kind of donation to their temple.[1] Groups which perform in the *banjar* building have to pay some amount of their income for hiring the set of musical equipment along with other 10 per cent of their total income for maintaining *banjar* building: especially the space, stage, chairs and light. Some groups divide money among their members every month.

Professional dancers and musicians in Ubud are always on demand, but they too find it difficult to live by performing for tourists alone. It is impossible to live a modern mode and style of life from the money one makes by performing for tourists, says the leader of "Gunungsari" group that has got almost nine decades long history of performing for tourists. "Many 'big' hotels are found forming own gamelan groups out of its staffs with the purpose of performing for tourists. Tourists in such case watch something produced or performed by less professional in a less Balinese atmosphere. Tourists do not bother to know if dancers and musicians are real professionals. There are some agencies which always block the meeting between and among 'real' performers and

1. A personal interview with I. Wayan Swatuma.

tourists,"[2] says Hendrawan. This shows that those who perform in the *banjar* buildings, temple yards and palace courtyard believe that they hold a better art and knowledge and can provide more "real" Balinese dance and drama to tourists than do the hotel-owned groups. A *Kecak* group usually is membered by over 150 performers. Similarly, there are in general seventy members in each *Legong* and *Barong* dance group. As mentioned above, several *banjar*-based groups donate all the money that they manage to allocate to the temple fund. A few of them after allocating their income to certain community fund divide money among their members every six months no matter how small the amount it may be. Mr. Dalem, the leader of "Tirta Sari" group told the researcher that his groups also perform for big hotels in Nusa Dua and Kuta, occasionally, and this brings good money to the artists. The more a group remain popular the more it is in demand, and so do remain the group members economically safe.

Many professional dancers and musicians work for offices of one or the other kind. Many of them run business of their own. They accept the fact that they lack time to rehearse new pieces therefore they feel comfortable to stage the ones that they are familiar with or used to. Ms. Ni Wayan Prilini who performs thrice a week in the *Puri* Ubud told the researcher that before she got married, she would perform six days a week and would draw 5,00,000 Rupiah (approximately US $ 56) per month. But these days she, a mother of two babies, runs a school for local kids. She can perform over a dozen dances but stages only a few of them for two groups. Artists interviewed agree that they do not feel fresh every time they come on the stage. The leader of "Bina Rameja" group articulates a fact that it is natural that sometimes, performers

---

2. A personal interview with Tjokorde Alit Hendrawan.

do not feel energy on the stage and some of them may count the number of audience. But every artist in the world wants to have lots of audience, "let's be frank about it."[3]

Professional performers especially the graduates from the ISI have managed to draw impressions from locals as well as tourists within a short span of time in Ubud. But forming a group out of professionals is criticized for being exclusive from within as well. Local instructors and group leaders argue that those professionals who dare to work with amateurs and learners make a meaningful contribution to their art and culture. "To form a group out of learners, amateurs, and professions is to see and go through an experience of an important order as one can see artists grow day by day like a plant," argues music instructor, Tjokorda Raka Swastika, a local Ubudian. Moreover, if performers come from the same community there are possibilities that they can have a greater mutual understanding. Mr. Swastika as a musician and instructor of women *gamelan* groups in Ubud believes that playing with "raw minds" is always difficult but very rewarding. Group formed out of professionals alone can draw money and popularity within a short period of time but such a group can lack "certain fundamental gravity."[4] Performing for tourist is criticized from within the community of performers as well. Putra, Bali's "number one" *Baris* dancer (Brochure), and also the leader of two performing groups argues that many professionals seem as if they are performing for money as they do not seem to perform with "love and feeling." He accepts a fact that there are many performers who are very good in dance and music but they too cannot

3. A personal interview with I. Wayan Roja.
4. A personal interview with Tjokorda Raka Swastika.

set some time to contemplate and rehearse, and thus are unable to produce more creative works since they remain busy as they perform for more than one group and are busy almost in works all days. They become prey to their own choices.[5]

Performing a Research on Ubud's Performance Culture

Researching on the performance culture practised for tourists in Ubud for me was an act of exploring my own self involved in understanding and writing about other's performance culture. Arguments put by the researchers and theorists like Norman K. Denzin that one cannot represent other's culture through producing research write-ups (1997: xi) but one's own self did problematize my position in Ubud too. The questions that the artists would ask me, now I take, were as important as the ones which I would often ask them. A women's *gamelan* group was going through the process of rehearsal throughout my stay in Ubud. Watching mostly the women performers rehearse for months before they would be allowed to perform for tourists on a regular basis made me realize the important contribution that they were making to Ubud's performance culture. The scene, I take as a metaphor of continuity and change state of Ubud's performance culture. Several times, I realized that the contribution that this women's *gamelan* group makes to the performance culture of Ubud remains far more important and powerful than the research that I was conducting (see *fig.* 6). I always felt a "little" while watching them rehearse their dance and musical compositions to meet the expectation of academics and local maestros.

First thing that struck me most about the Balinese in Ubud is that they took my being a "Hindu" from Nepal very seriously. They would advise me to introduce myself as a "Hindu from Nepal" at every ceremony that I would visit so

5. A personal interview with A.A. Putra.

that I could get into the temple and observe rituals minutely. But to my surprise, I would find several foreigners: Australians, Europeans and Americans, dressed in Balinese cultural attire already inside temple precincts and performing *pūjā* probably in a better manner than I did. Several times, I hesitated occupying the place among the Balinese Hindus seated in their ritualistic poses. I realized that their expression and gestures of offering were far more different and disciplined than mine. I could understand a few Sanskrit words that the priests would recite but I encountered completely different aura and semiotics of rituals that the Balinese Hindus carried out in their *pūjā*s in the temple. I must mention here that I a brāhmaṇa in my mid-thirties have either forgotten or ignored several rituals that my parents trained me to practise in my childhood days. I personally feel an outcaste in the Brāhmanic cultures in Nepal. Interestingly, Nepal had just declared itself a secular nation when I landed in Bali. Psychologically, I was in a euphoria state and felt politically liberated.

Several Balinese youths, some of them my friends now, would ask me to write down their names in the Sanskrit or *Devanāgarī* script. Many of them made stickers of their names in the *Devanāgarī* script and pasted on their bikes. They would ask me questions such as "does king Gyanendra read the Vedas?" I felt odd telling them that Hindu kings can become as worse and foolhardy as any dictators in the world. They were as emotional as I was about the 2001 Royal Palace massacre in Nepal. Many senior artists I interviewed would tell me that they have a dream of visiting Hindu temples and holy shrines in India and Nepal. They would talk about their neighbours who have been in his or her *tīrtha yātrā*, the holy pilgrimage to India. Many academicians in Bali I met would love to talk about the Indianizing process of the Balinese culture through the *Sāī-Bābā* and the *Kṛṣṇa Praṇāmī* cults among other contemporary Indian religious practices that are becoming popular among the Balinese Hindus.

Several times I was proposed to be a business partner as the local entrepreneurs had seen me walking down the streets everyday for months in Ubud. Several business offices in Ubud are run in joint venture entrepreneurship between Balinese and the Westerners. Leaders of performing groups I interviewed would expect me to write about their groups. They thought that my writing would go worldwide and would help them to promote their group's business. Many of them would expect me to stay at their homes as a paying guest.

I had seen and experienced the April 2006 people's uprising that brought an end to the age-old political system/monarchy in Nepal. Therefore, I was all politics when I landed in Bali. Conversley, I came across research articles that praised the *Puri* or the palace in Ubud for helping to preserve the local arts and cultures in Bali. Deep down, I longed to find some republicans and found that only a few bothered about politics in Ubud. Former princes are contesting elections held under the democratic political system, and importantly, they use their former roles of patronizing dance and drama in a new context and manner. They let the local performing groups perform in their palace courtyard; and since they also own hotels and restaurants they offer jobs to locals. They use their resources as a means of acquiring political power in a new social and cultural context of Indonesia. Politically, economically, culturally and intellectually, former princes are resourceful in Bali, for that matter, in Ubud too. Children of former princes also belong to a particular performing group and perform for tourists on a regular basis. Kathmandu especially the Newar performance culture in the Valley can never become like that of Ubud, a conclusion that I drew several times. But a possibility of creating a vibrant traditional Newar performance culture in Kathmandu, in a manner similar to the ways Balinese artists have invented in Ubud, kept me engaged into the research.

I met artists, researchers, academicians, former "hippies" among whom there were those who had been to Bali for the first time and those who had been there for over sixteen times, and still others who had been to Nepal too. Ubud as I experienced is full of life. Sometimes the person sipping coffee at the next table would turn out to be an installation artist from California or a professor emeritus from German university or a tourist who is curious to know what I was writing and reading about. Sometimes, Ubud would bore me especially when the person sitting at the next table in a café looked tired and unhappy, and did not accept me as a living being as it were. Taxi drivers down the streets would make me feel miserable as they would ask — god knows how many times — if I needed a taxi. Ubud becomes very noisy during the day. Boys ride bikes without silencer stretching one's nerves from the Nomad Restaurant to the Tourist Information Centre, in front of the *Puri* Ubud.

But Ubud is full of music throughout the evening. Procession of one or the other kind keeps on taking place, and temple ceremony of one or the other community keeps on happening. As over thousand artists in Ubud and around it perform for tourists every evening, an ephemeral world of gods, demons and nymphs evaporate as it were. There appears a Hanumān on his epic journey to find out Sītā; an age comes to an end after Rāma with the help of Hanūman and others kills the demon Rāvaṇa; the Kaurava and the Pāṇḍava bothers are seen fighting the same age-old but interesting battles; Abhimanyu, the son of Arjuna, meets the same fate at the end; Indra is lucky and clever enough this time too as he manages to send his brilliant and beautiful nymphs or *apsaras*es to break the penance of some courageous demon bothers; Lord Śiva is sick; Pārvatī is in a hurry to send her guards to get the medicine; *Barong* and *Rangda* are in a constant fight this time round too. Tourists/audiences keep on flashing on and off their cameras to arrest these very ephemeral worlds and creatures. And, as the night wanes, Ubud's sky starts to echo with the continuous melody of roasters till the morning. Ubud makes one feel proud of staying there. I personally feel that I was in the most beautiful place and researching about the most beautiful thing in this world — the Balinese dance and drama.

Importantly, several forces have contributed in the making of this performance culture, that the metropolitan audience from different parts of the world come to watch in Ubud, to come into function. And, watching the tourists in Ubud watch performances made for them, in fact, made me to follow some of the same trajectories which the performance culture in Ubud took to reach to this stage of continuity and change. Therefore, when one sits to watch and study the performances made for the tourists in Ubud, he or she simultaneously watches the invisible yet significant historical roles that the lovers and guardians of the Balinese art and culture did play at different times in the past which is the subject of the next chapter.

3

Makers and Maintainers of Images of Balinese Performance Culture

Balipedia and Tourism

BEFORE the artists, researchers and tourists around the globe started visiting Bali on a regular basis, i.e. since the beginning of the twentieth century, there were colonizers and their agents who had tried their best to exploit and vulgarize the art and culture of the Island. The images that the colonizers had created and circulated around the world slowly gave way to the power of the images which highlighted the Balinese performance art and culture in a newer and friendly manner. In course of times, the encounters of the Balinese art and culture with the world outside have become so recurrent that it is supposed to have created a great repertoire of discourses or archives also known as "Balipedia" now. Bali still keeps on drawing the attention of the scholars and tourists from around the globe, but especially of those artists, researchers, tourists and tourism business makers who visited Bali in the 1920s and 1930s are often taken as the historically important image-makers of Bali's performance art and culture. The images of Bali's nature and culture in the form of books, travelogues and photographs created by the individual researcher and traveller of the then period paved the way for the advent of tourism on a massive scale in the latter part of the twentieth century. Geoffrey Gorer, a writer who visited Bali in the first quarter of the year 1935 writes:

> The methods by which the missionaries tried to gain the Governor-General's permission to corrupt Bali are typical. The Balinese village is neat and orderly, but the roads are of earth, and after heavy tropical rain naturally look filthy. The missionaries took films of them in this condition, if necessary adding garbage of their own; they hired the poorest and most diseased people they could find to parade in these puddled streets, and exhibited in Europe these artificially sordid pictures as typical of Balinese life; and so worked on the feelings of the pious and humane to send monster petitions to the Governor-General, begging that the misery of such savages should be lighted by the good offices of the Lutheran Church. (1991: 57)

Importantly, Bali as an island that already consisted of several tiny kingdoms was going through some major historically important social and artistic transformations during the period between the Wars. The changes that were taking place in the Balinese societies, arts and cultures on the one hand, and the changes that were taking place in the very methodologies of understanding Bali's art and culture from outside on the other, did converse with spectacular results. Such convergence resulted in the creation of several newer images and discourses of Bali's art and culture. And the new images, no matter how exotic they were, reached out to a wider range of readers and lovers of Balinese art and culture through the very medium of tourism business and the print capitalism. Researchers on Bali hold a view that it was the second and the third decade of the last century when the images of Bali as "the island paradise really took hold" (Vickers 1989: 03). The images made in that period have got circulated around the world and have functioned as "reflective images of the past," which had "an intentional striving to replicate" (Valeri 1990: 155) now. The images of Bali's performance culture created in the then period have functioned as powerful *mantra*s since they have been revived by the tourism business makers of both national as well as international order in the present times. So much so, the images of Balinese art and culture created in the period between the wars have become so powerful that even if the academicians "like to think that they can challenge popular stereotypes in favour of more accurate assessments of society, the resurgence of the 1930s image of Bali as a paradise has gone ahead despite the recent increase in scholarly studies of Bali" (Vickers 1989: 189).

Several things have helped the Balinese performance culture to project its images to the world outside. Many Royalties and commoners from Bali fought the war known as "*poepoetan*" or "the self-sacrifice" against the Dutch Empire in 1906. This image of the epic and tragic grandeur made the colonial rulers "to develop a more worthy and tourism-friendly image of Bali" to "obliterate the memory of their brutal intervention" (Picard 1996: 20). Importantly, the period between the Wars was an important time in the history of Balinese dance and music as there lived artists who created the aesthetic revolution known as the *Kebyar*, discussed later, that directly helped Bali to project or cast images of its performance culture into multiple forms to the world outside. And then there arrived researchers and tourism business makers in Bali. Andre Roosevelt, the agent of the Thomas Cook, and Walter Spies, the first and the important researcher on the Balinese performing art and culture in the 1920s, would discourage the local Balinese leaders not to buy cars and construct their house of iron roofs. Particularly, Roosevelt would say to some local leaders: "The white man has started schools. That coolie boy, if he is clever, may become the chief in twenty years from now. Democracy is slowly creeping in. Do you like that?" And, of course, they did not, for they know that a democratic government in Bali would be prosperous"

(Roosevelt 1989: xv-xvi). Roosevelt further writes, he and Spies wanted to make Bali a "national or international park, with special laws to maintain it as such" (Roosevelt 1989: xvi).

The *Colonial Exposition* of Balinese traditional dance and drama, the world famous event, took place in Paris in 1931. It provided Balinese dance and drama academically an important recognition among the European audience and theatre creators and critics. Several pieces of the period such as the *Gong* dance, the *Kebyar*, and the *janger* choreographed or created in the 1920s were staged on the occasion. Though critics and audiences in Europe received it as the traditional Balinese dance and drama forms, several of them were "purely recreational" *janger* rather than one of the "most sacred and mysterious rituals" that impressed Artaud" (2003: 255), writes Sergio Costola.

The Importance of Being Image Creators

Walter Spies, Collin McPhee, Rudolf Bonnet and Margaret Mead among other scholars did not only research and produce texts on Balinese art and culture but also influenced many local art practitioners as well as foreign researchers who would work to promote Balinese art and culture in the latter part of the twentieth century. Every touristically famous place in Bali now holds some historical associations with the individual visitor and researcher who came, set business and stayed in Bali during the period between the wars. Ubud is associated with Walter Spies, Rudolf Bonnet and Collin McPhee. Spies and McPhee were musician and painter. They wrote works on Bali, and influenced Balinese performance culture tremendously as they "developed and marketed to Europe and America Ubud's first and most enduring export product: the image of Bali as a natural, social, and aesthetic paradise" (MacRae 1992; Vickers 1989: 95-130).

Walter Spies himself wrote, "The harmony of Balinese life has been achieved" (Zeote and Spies 1986: 3). Mead wrote that Bali has got "living art, that the music, the dance, the theatre, despite their high degree of stylization, are nevertheless extremely alive, constantly being recreated in hundreds of performance all over the island" (1970: 145). Louis Couperus, a tourist of the same period wrote that he who loved ancient things in oriental surroundings could see them for himself in Bali (1994: 16). Powel, the canonizer of Bali as "the last paradise," found "the end and aim of living" in the music and dance he encountered in the island. His soliloquy: "Snap the camera shut! To hell with photographs and naked ladies. No film can catch the glamour of this moment. No gelatine can tell the music of the gamelan, the bursts of colour, the swirling tide of human piety" (1989: 216) makes one to realize the kind of aesthetic shock, intervention and wonder that these travellers who came here with touristic images of Bali might have been through then. Zoete and Spies further writes,

> We gaze and gaze with an earnestness of purpose which fatigues us long before the dance is over. The Balinese, like other orientals, enters into the atmosphere of the dance and remains there as in a familiar landscape. (1986: 16)

Thus it was narrated to the listeners and readers around the globe that the Balinese delighted "in the art of acting rather than in the play, in the way in which the music is played rather than in the music, in the mechanics of the green room rather in the play itself . . ." (Mead 1970: 343).

Similarly, for the tourists who visited Bali in the period between the Wars, the inhabitants and culture of Bali became "incredible as it may seem, inconceivably beautiful," "as beautiful as one can imagine." Balinese women for them became "a physiological simple and dignified beauty" and "full of Eastern nobility and natural chastity." And, finally such image-maker of Bali was furious with his god that "he was not born in Bali" (Krause qtd. in Picard 1996: 30). Such images, after they were disseminated in the world of tourism business, became very powerful simulacra and they kept on floating. Their signified were affirmed by the tourists and the agents of the tourism business makers in and outside Bali as well: "I went there half-unwillingly" and "convinced that I had seen the nearest Utopia that I am ever to see." Gorer further writes:

> In Bali I saw the only happy large community I have seen in my life, and I have tried to analyse for myself and others how this happiness is brought about and maintained, and have tried to apply my conclusions to the conditions around me. Perhaps more able people will re-do the task and reach more practical conclusions. For I do not want to think of the happiest community that I know half of the world away in another hemisphere. I want it in the streets outside my door.
> (1991: 108-9)

Tourists as they started to arrive in hundreds every year since 1920s saw Bali as a perfect example of an oriental mode of living and performance culture. Tourists would find more than what the agents of tourism business would promise them to get. Margaret Mead writes that though the agents of tourism business in the West in the 1930s advertised Bali using the "slim figure of a high-breasted, scantily clothed girl" as luring images, even those tourists visiting for three days only found the air in Bali "never empty of music" (Mead 1970: 332-33). The Balinese performance culture surprised tourists and researchers alike. Bali "induced in us a vision of a profoundly creative popular culture in which art and life, at least, some place, genuinely are one" (1983: 52) wrote Clifford Geertz.

Spies and Zoete write that Balinese have dance and music suited to every occasion, an appropriate type of gamelan for every mode of rites: birthdays, tooth filling, weddings, cremations, for temple feasts and processions to the sea with the holy images, for purifications and the driving away of disease and demons (1970: 262-63). For many travellers and researchers encountering the Balinese performance culture was an intervention into their own Western metropolitan mode of experiencing art and culture. They saw "the warming air in Bali spangled with shimmering jets of sound" which to their wonder and happiness sounded as "oriental music should sound — like muffled laughter of forgotten gods" (Powel 1989: 5). Powel further writes, "I drink the sound. It pours like drops of crystal pattered in a cloth of beads" (1989: 215). McPhee wrote that each night as the music started up "I experienced the same sensation of freedom and indescribable freshness" (2002: 40). Zoete and Spies write that watching dancing for the Balinese is not "of such concentrated attention as with us. It is almost a state of being, a feeling rather than an action" (1986: 16). For Powel watching the musician playing gamelan in Bali was to experience an ecstatic moment as musicians and music would become "a single organism, merged in something greater than themselves" and the atmosphere of watching the performance itself to him was "fleshless ecstasy, the end and aim of life," "distillate of being" and "bloodless merging with the eternal Brahm" (1989: 215-16). Thus much depended on those who visited Bali between the period of the wars and the kind of images they produced of Balinese performance culture. Luckily, the travellers and the researchers of the period were some of the great admirers of the Balinese art and culture as well as writers who could articulate new modes of aesthetic experience effectively.

Similarly, a tourist in Bali in the past had to walk through several trails, rice fields and villages before he or she would arrive at the venue to watch the performance. Experiences that he or she would undergo through the state of pre-performance, performance and post-performance stages stimulated him or her to articulate images accordingly. Tourists of the 1950s had to travel thirty miles through "a narrow winding road" at "velvety black night" down the paddy fields which "flooded with water and into the recesses of jungle gorges" and amidst the "nocturnal slumbering" of monkeys and their "chattered and shrieked" sounds (Clune and Stephensen 1994: 246) before they would arrive at the venue and become audience of the *Kecak* performance. Clune and Stephenson articulate the experience of watching a *Kecak* performance in the 1950s in the following manner:

> On the floor of the bowl, in the temple-court, a phalanx of crouching bodies were huddled in a ring. They were motionless, and expectant. A chill ran down my spine, at some undefined terror, hidden in jungle, waiting to strike. The dim forms, massed in the silent darkness, were like spirits in the eternal night of Chaos before creation. From the outer darkness a torch-bearer approached, carrying aloft a fire-stick glowing with resinous flame. We saw about 200 brown men, girdled only by loin-cloths, squatting in serried circles on the hot damp earth, their eyes downcast. The torch-bearer broke through the circles towards a giant wooden candelabrum, with branches like a tree. He illuminated its torches, which flared and cast a vivid flickering light. A tense silence descended, broken only by the eerie screech of monkeys in the distant tree tops. As though at this signal, the drama began. The bodies of the men packed in the serried circles grew rigid. Then, like a thunder-lightning clap which rends a tree in twain, the silence was split by a sudden single hand-clap and yell of 200 voices in unison warning of danger. (Clune and Stephensen 1994: 246-47)

This narration or description about the *Kecak* performance that the writers saw has achieved universality as it were in the recent years partly because of the power of the writing itself and partly because this narration has come to fulfill the need of the tourism and the cultural policy makers of Bali/Indonesia, finally it addresses the need of the performing groups as their brochures heavily borrow words from the text cited above.

The Western image-makers of the Balinese arts and cultures were also the inventors of the tourism culture in Bali. Walter Spies is often credited for playing a major role in turning Balinese local artists into "professional" by "helping them to direct their works towards the budding tourist market" (Picard 1996: 32) especially in Ubud. Similarly, Katharane and Jack Mershon, the German Neuhaus brothers and the Belgian aristocrat Adrien Le Mayeur de Merpres are credited for making Sanur a famous place for tourism in Bali. Kuta Beach, the first hotel in Kuta, now the most touristic and crowded place in Bali, was built by an American, Robert Koke, and his English American partner (Vickers 1989: 109). These researchers and business makers in Bali of those days now evoke the mythic, spiritual and cultural roles played by R̥ṣi Mārkaṇḍeya. R̥ṣi Mārkaṇḍeya was a famous sage from the classical Indic time and space, who is believed to have given Bali a new lease of spiritual and cultural life of different order and nature in the eighth century. These talents of the West helped to set and create places that would in later days become famous zones of tourism of global scales in Bali. Such transformations in tourism business in Bali have made the Balinese performance culture and spirituality which were supposed to have been installed or originated by R̥ṣi Mārkaṇḍeya to become more spectacular in the present times. Walter Spies was a *guru* to many trendsetter researchers and artists in Bali, and he lived in Ubud, and "Bali was chosen — partly as a result of the image developed in Ubud and exported all over the world during the 1930s — as the central locale for this development" (MacRae 1999: 137-38). Interpreted through neo-historical point of view, these travellers and researchers on Bali in the period between the Wars acted out the persona of the mythic character, Ṛṣi Mārkaṇḍeya by giving a new dynamism to the art and culture set by the latter as the myth goes.

Besides, expats too have played an important role in promoting the images that the former tourists and researchers in Bali had created in the past. Expats in Bali often narrate their experience in a similar manner that the tourists of the past would do. They appreciate the dance and drama staged in temple premises on cultural occasions but blame the same dance performed by the same dancer for tourists as lacking some fundamental qualities in it. They use their experience of watching Balinese dance, drama and musical forms performed on the occasion of the festivals and rituals as tropes of power acquired by encountering 'authentic' Balinese performance culture. Since they have lived in Bali as expats for decades, they are well known and are respected by local leaders and guardians, and are invited to attend several temple ceremonies held in the communities. As they go through such experience and opportunities, expats in Bali live or act out the persona that was lived and performed by Spies and McPhee among other researchers on the Bali of the past times.

The futuristic plan of the 1970s and 1980s, discussed in brief later in this chapter, interestingly evoked the past of Bali as the write-ups produced on the Balinese art and culture in the period between the Wars and their producers got different prominence in the post-1970s in Bali. The New Order of Soeharto and entrepreneurs around the globe brought back the memories of Spies and his friends. And Spies and his colleagues' works and their personas became more prominent as the tourism business and culture in Bali started to flourish.

Moreover, contemporary tourism business is supposed to have brought a greater cultural and spiritual awareness among the locals in Bali in such a way that the mythic past of Bali has become a trope of survival in a global future. Balinese are thanked for moving "into the future by returning to their past, and embrace modernity by reacquainting themselves with old traditions" (Howe 2001: 83). As the tourism business in Bali was set to make the adventure of an international scale in the 1970s, the revival and circulation of the older images of Bali and its art and culture took place in a fast pace. Vickers writes that the former generations of expatriate residents from the 1930s wrote or republished their works. Travel agencies used the images created by these writers and travellers. Moreover, Sukarno's nation-building, Suharto's development policies, local elites' concerns (1989: 4, 176) and the views of "the Dutch orientalists and American anthropologists, the artists and tourists converged" (Picard 1996: 38) to make tourism business successful in Bali. In no time did Bali become an important island in the independent Indonesia and the Balinese performance culture surprised the cultural and tourism policy makers not only of Indonesia but also of the world around.

Kebyar Images of the Balinese Performance Culture

The Western researchers in Bali during the period between the Wars encountered one of the most important transitional phases that the Balinese dance, drama and musical forms were going through. Covarrubias, who lived in Bali for a couple of years in the mid-1930s wrote that the leaders or musician maestros of the "Gong Ringdikit" from North Bali came to Belaluan and taught "the dynamic and revolutionary style of the north" and also "learned the classical pieces of the south" and similarly, the musicians of Belaluan "went to other villages to break in new organizations and were always lavishly entertained" (1972: 210). McPhee directly encountered the societal and aesthetic transformations that were taking place in Bali of that period too. He writes, on the one hand "glittering court life was almost a thing of the past," but on the other "the village music rang more loudly than ever" as a new wave of "musical enthusiasm had recently swept the island, and clubs formed overnight as young musicians organized to learn Kebyar" (2001: 30-31). Bandem and deBoer write that the intense rivalry between the villages, Bungkulan and Jagaraga in North Bali in the domain of creating new musical and dance compositions on a regular basis gave birth to the modern Balinese aesthetic phenomenon called *Kebyar.* They further write, "Played at blinding speed, with sudden violent shifts of témpo and volume, it sounds much more energetic than the older forms of gamelan music" (1995: 75). This form of aesthetic revolution swept in a cultural renaissance in Bali (Miettinen 1992: 135). And, in no time, and for every one's joy, "Kebyar style became the lingua franca of Balinese music as no other type of orchestral repertoire had before" (Tenzer 1991: 23-24).

Importantly, Walter Spies can be taken as the right person in the right time and place as he was a musician and researcher who could observe social and aesthetic changes that Balinese dance and drama forms were going through very pertinently. He records the process of how some simple Balinese musical forms became "complicated by different effects of orchestration," "certain instruments were suppressed and others introduced, till a new gamelan, the Gong Kebyar, obtained an independent existence," as a result, players sat "facing each other across space about eight feet square which is the stage of the Kebyar dancer" (Zoete and Spies 1986: 233). This is regarded as a very important change in the formalistic and the thematic structures of the musical forms. Up to the time *Kebyar* took over Bali, the music created "a mood, an ambience; it filled the space with gentle notes and embraced the listener" but Kebyar style music and dance "pervaded the space in an aggressive way" (Dibia and Ballingar 2004: 22-23).

And, the *Kebyar* phenomenon, in no time, enabled individual talents to create and practise dances in newer themes and styles. I. Made Bandem writes that almost every decade of the twentieth century saw newer developments in *Kebyar* dance in Bali. Solo male dances which were popular in the beginning of the twentieth century gave rise to the practice of solo female dances later, and then came the duet dances which set ground for group dances that would first depict the romantic subject. Then came the social and political themes and lately, the romantic world of birds and animals (2006: 1-12). This aesthetic revolution that the Balinese dance, drama and musical forms have gone through can be linked to the observation of Walter Sorrel that dances have their "sociological and historic connotations. They often foreshadow a new cultural trend. As soon as a dance reflects its age, the folk dance material has by then gone through a process of refinement" (1967: 72-3).

The *Kebyar* phenomenon in Balinese dance and music brought varieties within as individual talents from different communities in Bali started practising or inventing dances in newer styles and paved the way for the performance culture of a greater magnitude. Individual Balinese talents like Mario (*Mah-ree-yhe*) from Tabanan area took the Balinese scene by storm (Tenzer 1991: 78) in the period between 1920s and 1950s. Mario's genius gave the *Kebyar* of the South Bali its unique quality (Zoete and Spies 1986: 233). Moreover, the tourists and the researchers who came in the period between the Wars met Mario and watched him as a performer as well as a trainer. They regarded Mario as the living metaphor of the Balinese performance culture of that period. Mario became the hero of the first half of the twentieth century among the villagers as well as researchers and tourists from abroad in Bali. He was seen creating new dance and drama pieces. He was variously met as a young man, sick man and an old man who was seen training children. He was seen "marking the musical accents with the pupil's body" and almost wrestling with the little body "pressing the music into its limbs" (Zoete and Spies 1986: 31). Covarrubias watched the regular weekly performance of Mario in the hotel yard. He writes, "Mario straightened like a startled cobra, tense and nervous, holding the fan over his head as if to shade his eyes" and with half-closed eyes "he swayed from left to right, his elbows almost touching the mat, fanning himself or deftly arranging the flowers on his head-dress with quivering fingers" (1972: 233). Joan Coast writes, "Mario's eyebrows did not flutter with great speed — he hinted, rather, that he was raising them, very gently and with the most subtle innuendo; and a split second after his eyes had started out his head they relaxed back into a suggestion of quite urchin humour but only a suggestion. Without that supremely mobile face and its quality of unconscious greatness, no other dancer could hope to compare with Mario" (1954: 91). Mario, the metaphor of the *Kebyar* phenomenon, unknowingly became the cultural ambassador of the Balinese performance culture abroad. Tourists and researchers who met Mario, and watched and wrote about his performance made him world famous. But as a genius Mario lived the life of a dancer, and believed "If I had smelled blood at a fight (cockfight), I would dance better" (Mario qtd. in Coast 1954: 104).

Locals as Maintainers of Images

Tourism business and local performance cultures together form a topic for a contested discourse of an important nature especially in this era over the issue of globalization. Local cultures become a subject of great importance in the tourism business because some cultural services provided for tourists "cannot be provided anywhere: they have to be produced and consumed in very particular places" (Urry 2002: 38). Similarly, the tidal wave of tourism business somewhere is taken as not strong enough to damage local cultures. For example, the "fabric of Balinese society" is taken as "too strong and too flexible to be rent by easy money" (Elegant 1987: 9). Moreover, every change in local culture brought in by tourism business and culture is also taken as the "continuous process of cultural change" (Cohen 1984: 388), and Bali is taken as a proof of it.

Tourism business is supposed to have brought tremendous changes in Bali's local cultures. Before Kuta became famous for tourism, Putu Setia writes, "the ritual materials needed for offerings in temple on a daily basis would be prepared by family members, but now such materials are made by professionals and sold in the market — thus a subject of both regression and progress" (1994: 75). Tourism business has defined places in Bali in terms of the services that the latter could provide to tourists. Kuta known for surfing and night life is not a place for observing culture and ceremonies of local nature but a place where tourists perform "their own culture: drinking alcohol, listening to disco music, and having free intercourse" and "religious ceremonies do not rate a glance from the tourists in Kuta" (Setia 1994: 77). Similarly, Ubud is being defined as a tourist place where tourists are told that they will find themselves in a state of peace, and they can experience "another" or "real" Bali. "The *kebayas*, *sarongs* and myriad ways of tying *udengs* and *saputs*, funerary accoutrements, phantasmagoric and giant papier-mâché *ogoh-ogoh* effigies prepared to mark the Balinese New year and bamboo penjor masterpieces that festoon the village's streets during Galungan all make Ubud and its people stand tall"

(2004: 41), write Cody and Shwaiko. And these transformations that have taken place in the performance culture of Ubud do have direct relationship with the number of tourists who arrive here in Ubud everyday to watch performances staged for them.

Post-colonial and independent Indonesia introduced a master plan with an aim to galvanize the various strands of the budding tourism business in Bali. The plan document known as the *Bali Tourism Study* was finished in 1971 and approved by the World Bank in 1974. It was "the most important policy document on tourism in Bali" (McCarthy 1994: 14). This project was a mega-dream "to capture the manna of tourism and envious of Bali's privileged position" (Picard 1996: 45), and was prepared by French consultants and sponsored by the United Nations Development Program (UNDP) and the International Bank for Reconstruction and Development. It was a mega-adventure that was estimated to address 7,34,000 tourists a year. And, it, as an adventure of such scale, promised to provide the tourists of that hypothetical number a service worth US $35 per day. Thus it was decided that 9,500 rooms should be made in the seaside near the airport, removed from the local population. As a result, 6950 rooms were made at Nusa Dua and the remaining 2,550 rooms at Sanur, Kuta and Denpasar (Picard 1996: 45-6, McCarthy 1994: 14). It was decided to integrate the tourism business of this mega scale with the local Balinese cultures through the creation of opportunities for tourists to watch performances in certain places according to a time table suitable to them (Picard 1996: 46, McCarthy 1994: 14). Great care was taken to make tourists believe that in addition to the natural beauty, the island has also got its great heritage of living arts and cultures. "Attendance at performances is considered to be an indispensable part of a vacation in Bali. The dance could not remain unaffected by the inundation" (1995: 127), write Bandem and deBoer.

Finally, the national and the international agencies of the tourism business in Bali of the 1970s and 1980s decided to make the locals in Bali aware about the relationship between their performance culture and tourism business. The authorities in Bali devised the policy of "cultural tourism" (*pariwisata budaya*) that aimed to develop tourism without debasing the Balinese culture (Picard 1999: 15-16). This national goal offered new roles to the age-old village organization such as *banjar* and *desa*, especially the custodians of the local performance cultures, discussed in the next chapter, as they set to form groups with the purpose of performing for tourists and intensify their ceremonies into spectacular forms. Thus a role was offered to the locals especially those from Ubud to maintain the images of Balinese performance culture in a newer socio-economic context.

Canonizers of Balinese Dance and Drama

The researchers and travellers of the first half of the twentieth century were surprised for not finding any dance schools in Bali. McPhee, the world famous musicologist writes that instructors in Bali are professional or retired dancers who have specialized in only one form of their art (2002: 308). This traditional mode of disseminating dance and drama was taken as proof of a living culture that induced in researchers mainly of the West "a vision of a profoundly creative popular culture in which art and life, at least, at some place, genuinely are one" (Geertz 1983: 52). But great many changes have taken place in Bali's academic world since then. Academy has not only made its four-decade long history but has also brought many changes in the performance culture of Bali. When university in Bali started to offer courses on the Balinese dance and music, it was first "viewed with about," but nowadays taking such academic course "is simply assumed that a serious young musician should get a formal education if he or she plans to earn an income" (Tenzer 1991: 25). However, coming to the academic styles, "officially sanctioned, standard dance versions" are criticized for replacing "local variations" which hold important history and origin of "diffusion of particular artistic styles from one part of Bali to another" (Hough 1999: 249).

The state-run academia in Bali is appreciated for taking "the role of patronage previously held by the princely courts: the creation of styles and the establishments of standards of execution; the training of dancers and musicians; and the organizations and financing of performances" (Picard 1996: 170-71). The academia in Bali is also credited for producing a "civil service elite" of younger generation coming from "different villages or areas in Bali with long artistic traditions" (Vickers 1989: 208-9). It is supposed to have set "the future of the arts in Bali, and of culture as a whole. Its equivalents in the religious sphere are the government and private organizations which debate, sponsor and decide on the direction Balinese religion should take" (Vickers 1989: 208-9). Bandem, the former director of ASTI/STSI/ISI, and deBoer write that the academies in Bali have played an important role in the development of modern performing dance and musical forms as "A number of choreographers and composers have made their debut creations which are picked up by village-based artists or groups" (1995: 135-39). Moreover, ISI as an important academic centre in Bali encourages composers to "collaborate with other musicians and performance artists from all over the world" (Dibia and Ballinger 2004: 16).

Academics in Bali are aware of a strong heritage of local dance and drama of various forms. They find it very important to address "how the styles of different regions place a different emphasis on choreographic posture (*agem*), movement phrases (*tandang*) and movement transitions (*tangkis*)" (Herbest 1997: 98). Many local dance and drama forms and styles are still associated with the local maestros of the past. A.A. Gde Mandera of Peliatan is known for *Legong Keraton Peliatan* style, I Gst. Gde Raka is known for his *legong saba* style, and Kakul is known for *gambuh Batuan* style. Their styles are the proofs that "Balinese dance style can be distinguished from the dance forms following the different technique and aesthetic aspects as well as the local style/individual master's style" (Swasthi Bandem 2004: 62-63). This aesthetic consciousness has made local artists or *seniman alam* always in demand as they are requested to take practical classes in art colleges. But due to the ever increasing number of students enrolled in the art colleges it has become almost impossible to train students thoroughly. Hough, a former non-Indonesian student of the ISI writes that graduates in the college "received a more thorough training (particularly in classic forms) than it is now possible to provide — given the constraints of time, the larger number of the students, and the demands of the curriculum" (1999: 246). On the other hand, performing groups from Peliatan openly defy, discussed in the fifth chapter, the influence of academia, for that matter the ISI-styled dance and drama forms. They feel a sense of duty and prestige in maintaining their own local forms of music and dance. They argue that the ISI does not need to worry about its creations but the artists from Peliatan have many reasons to worry about their dance and musical forms because if they do not maintain their local heritage, no one else will bother about doing it.

Importantly, the Balinese performance culture since the early years of the 1970s has become a subject of academic and bureaucratic interventions. Academy in Bali for the first time set out to define and divide Balinese dances into sacred and secular forms or images in the 1970s. Balinese dance and drama forms were categorized in terms of the audience who watch them. If they are watched by tourists they become secular, otherwise they remain sacred. This methodology of categorizing traditional Balinese dance, drama and musical forms is taken as a part of the development of modern Balinese aesthetics. Though invented by academicians and cultural policy makers, the demarcation line between and among the sacred, the ceremonial and the secular has worked as a trope of powerful intervention into the Balinese performing arts and culture within, and has generated aesthetic consciousness accordingly. However, this academic and bureaucratic intervention is often criticized for creating differences which were not there before. Traditional dance and drama in Bali have remained an important and essential part of the macro-world that Balinese have lived since time immemorial. It is argued that Balinese "do not see sharp qualitative differences between spiritual and material, or supernatural and natural, or between God and humanity. Rather they stress the inadequacy of our human knowledge of those aspects of the universe that are normally intangible" (Hildred Geertz 1992: 8). Similarly, Balinese are defined as people who do not bother to "separate the supernatural from the natural. The spirit world is a living force that must be recognized and appeased through rituals and offerings" (Slattun 1992: 12).

This need to draw demarcation line between and among the Balinese traditional dance and drama forms emanated after it was found that dances that could be performed only on ritual occasions were also staged for the tourists. A seminar entitled "Sacred and Profane Dance" took place just before the publication of the "Master Plan for the Development of Tourism in Bali." The goal of this seminar was to "separate the "sacred art" (*seni sacral*) from (*seni provan*) and to decide which of the "sacred" forms could be commercialized" (Worsley 1995: 10). This exercise of categorizing Balinese dance and drama into "sacred art" (*seni sacral*) and "profane art" (*seni provan*) was "semantic borrowing" that "resulted in some awkward attempts on the part of the participants to forge a distinction that was foreign to them" (Picard 1996: 152-53). And, this academic exercise itself went through the process of reinterpretation when the Department of Religion put a suggestion to add one more category. Thus it was defined that the *bebali*, the entertaining dances would be considered *wali*, sacred when they "contributed to the completion of a ceremony," and same dance will be called secular or *balih-balihan* "when they were presented as mere entertainment" (Worsley 1995: 12). But this academic exercise of dividing Balinese dance and drama into three categories: *Seni tari wali* (sacred, religious dances), *Seni tari bebali* (ceremonial dances), and *Seni tari balih-balihan* (secular dances) has created "a new set of problems" (Picard 1996: 153-56). Moreover, the LISTIBIA, a governmental organization having a root to this context of academic and bureaucratic intervention has been given a task of approving the performances meant for staging for tourists in Bali and abroad. It has often become a subject of criticism for becoming biased on several decisions, and not being able to understand the dynamics of local Balinese dance and drama forms and styles.

However, it has surprised academicians and bureaucrats alike to find themselves sitting next to tourists while watching several important ritualistic performances carried out according to the Balinese cultural calendar. Ritualistic performances though are not performed for tourists in hotel yards, yet they can be watched by tourists. The *Berutuk* regarded as the "authentic" ritualistic dance and drama that "involves bachelors into rigorous ritual for almost one and a half months" (Bandem and deBoer 1995: 10) has now become a great occasion that brings tourists, bureaucrats and scholars together. Thus this intervention into the Balinese performance culture has created several other problems as Balinese themselves find it hard to separate which dance is sacred and which one is not. Under one rubric called "Baris" dance, there are multiple forms varying from the most sacred that is performed in the inner sanctum of temple to the ones that are performed with the purpose of entertaining not only tourists but also locals. And, it is difficult to decide which dance is secular and which is not. "Unlike the *wali* dances, those of the *bebali* type do not compel the god's attention, nor are they a necessary part of the ritual embedded in the performance. They are, nonetheless, explicitly religious in intention (1995: 26)," write Bandem and deBoer. Similarly, many Balinese contemporary dance and drama forms defy the demarcation lines discussed above. *Janger*, an entertaining dance form invented in the early period of the last century has now been taken as sacred after its performers were found going through the state of *nadi* or trance. "As a matter of fact, government officials became so embarrassed at these repeated "unscheduled" trances that they prohibited the group's janger performances" (1997: 130), writes Herbest. Thus the academic exercises invented and followed by authorities, on the one hand, and the very nature of the Balinese performance culture, on the other hand, have been caught in an interesting tussle as while the former strives to "disenchant" the world, the dancers in search of inspiration continue to evolve in an "enchanted" world" (Herbest 1996: 161).

Since it is mandatory that groups formed to perform for tourists need to take permission from the LISTIBIYA, locals regard it as a highly important bureaucratic and academic authority. I visited the *mesakapan*, a ritual ceremony conducted to mark the marriage between the musicians and their instruments organized for a women's gamelan group on 19 February 2007 (see *fig.* 7). The occasion consisted of several rounds of rituals carried out by the priests and the musicians on the stage for hours, and was followed by a performance that was watched by the local leaders, maestros and the representative of the LISTIBIYA (see *fig.* 8).

Tjokorda Ngurah Suyadnya, Wakil Legislatif from the *Puri* Saraswati Ubud, the representative of the LISTIBIYA, arrived just in time to watch the performance, and later discussed about the quality of the performance with the artists, local leaders and maestros. It was this representative who was also expected to give a name to the group. I was told by Suyadnya on 18 March 2007, one day before the Balinese New Year (Nyepi), that he had already found a name, but the group still had to go through rehearsal for several more months. The LISTIBIYA seems to have created hegemony among the artists who perform for the tourists in Ubud as they need to go through a process of negotiation regarding the quality of the performance as well as permission to stage shows at home and abroad. Senior artists from Peliatan though do not hesitate to criticize academic influence and forms especially those created by the ISI, they do not openly criticize the LISTIBIYA. Moreover, the representative who visited and checked the performance mentioned above was not an outsider but someone who is familiar with the regular progress of the local women performers.

Thus academics and bureaucrats have taken the responsibility of maintaining the heritage of the performance culture in the changed cultural context of Bali. This has given to some canons that demand many performers or the custodians of the performance cultures from Ubud and around to behave accordingly.

Old or New Images?

Tourism in Bali "crowned" the Balinese women as "queen" and "ornaments" of Balinese performing arts in its beginning days (Cok Sawitri 2001: 134). Now the question comes — will the old images of Bali and its performance culture keep on working especially in the present context when many groundbreaking achievements have been made by the Balinese women performers? Women *gamelan* groups have given a new energy to the Balinese performance culture at contemporary times. *Gamelan Wanita* (women's gamelan) has comparatively a shorter historicity. Historians regard Ni Ketut Suryatini as the founder of the first women's *gamelan* group in 1980 in Bali. They take Desak Suarti Laksmi as the first female teacher who taught Balinese *gamelan* music abroad and composed numerous pieces. Similarly, Desak Nyoman Suarti and Ni Gusti Putu Astiri are credited for creating a bigger space for women performers as they formed the "Topeng group" of all female members. "Mekar Sari women's gamelan" from Peliatan is credited for becoming the first women's group that started performing for tourists on a regular basis. Similarly, Ni Ketut Trijata and Ni Ketut Nondri have become world famous female *dalang*s or puppeteers, a domain that belonged to the Balinese males only in the past.

Several social and cultural forces have brought women artists into prominence in Bali at the present times. The Balinese women artists are breaking the clichéd images which the tourism in Bali in the past had made about them and projected into the world outside. Since the event "Gong Kebyar

Competition" also called "Mṛdaṅga Utsava" started to take place in Denpasar in 1968 annually, the participation of women's *gamelan* groups has become a matter of pride and joy for each region in Bali. All eight regencies in Bali take the participation of their women *gamelan* group in "Bali Art Festival" as a matter of pride and identity. In Ubud, three "Women Gamelan Groups" perform for tourists on a regular basis. This contemporary trend of "womanization" of the Balinese performing art has been ideologically and aesthetically counter-argued by all-men *arja* troupe that aimed "to show that there is something in the voice and body of males that make Balinese performance culture unique" (Sawitri 2001: 135). It is argued that the domination of women performers has made Balinese performing art "more sensual" and "aesthetically shallow" (Kadek Suardan and Sawitri 2001: 135).

Finally, the nature of tourism business in Bali is going through a process of change as the number of the Asian tourists to Bali has increased in the recent years. Japan has become the most-tourist-coming-nation to Bali since 2001. Out of the most tourist coming nations to Bali, six of them are Asian. This makes us ponder over the images which the tourism business and cultural policy makers in Bali will come with in future. Will the same older or traditional images of Balinese art and culture remain intact? Or will Balinese performance culture remain stronger by changing and renewing its traditions? Will the belief that the Balinese performance culture no longer remain as "a simple obstacle to social change, and especially to that particularly wished-for sort of social change called 'development'" (Geertz 1984: 2), a view taken by anthropologists move with new thrills?

Several forces and factors such as researchers, academia, locals, nation state, tourists of the past and the present, and tourism business makers have constructed and disseminated the images of the Balinese performing art and culture. But the participation of the locals in promoting their traditional art and cultural forms through the process of regular performance is the most remarkable feature of the contemporary Balinese performance culture in Ubud which is the subject of the next chapter.

4

Performing for Tourists
Blamed and Defended

History

THIS culture of performing for tourists in Bali has already carved out over a nine-decade long history. Tourists in the past could watch traditional Balinese dance and drama staged for them in hotel yards only, but they can watch them in the community buildings and courtyard of palace and temple now. Picard writes, "After the opening of the Bali Hotel by the KPM (Royal Packet Navigation Company) in 1928, these performances became a regular attraction, presented every Friday evening to the tourists freshly disembarked from Buleleng, and a pavilion was built with this purpose on the terrace of the hotel" (1996: 140-41). Similarly, McPhee writes of the year 1931 when tourists would watch dance performance at hotel at 9 p.m. (2002: 17). Zobel, a tourist in Bali in the mid-1920s of the last century who watched a performance organized for him and his wife, the only audience of the show, writes, "The dance took place in our courtyard and weird music had already been sounding there for an hour" (1994: 194). Covarrubias, a researcher on Balinese art and culture in the mid-1930s writes, "[W]e were fully prepared to hear another of the denatured versions of native entertainment usually concocted for tourists" (206). But once Covarrubias and his fellow tourists sat to watch the show, they found a "pure music" performed by one of the finest gamelans in Bali of the then period (1972: 206-07). Such performances worked as a 'pressure' and 'opportunity' for the Balinese local artists since they set to create new forms of dance and drama with the purpose of performing for tourists: "A 'Barong' performance was created by the local talents, I. Made Kredek and I. Wayan Geria in 1948 upon the request of the Bali Hotel in Denpasar" (Bandem and deBoer 1995: 131).

This culture of performing for tourists, though begun first at hotel yards, went through some major processes of transformation as tourists started walking all the way to villages with the purpose of watching performances designed and staged for them from the 1950s onwards. Clune and Stephensen, as cited in the previous chapter, describe the *Kecak* performance that they watched in the Bono village in the mid-1950s. From the 1960s onwards, performing for tourists became a *banjar* or community-based activity in many villages in Bali. The Peliatan-based *Kecak* group named "Samera Madya," established in 1966 was the first *banjar* or community-based group in Peliantan, and regards itself as the second commercial *Kecak* group in Bali after the one from the Bono village. The courtyard of the *Puri Agung*, Peliatan where "Samera Madya" stages the *Kecak* performance even these days holds important historicity of staging Balinese dance and drama forms of various natures for locals as well as tourists. Alit Dalem, the group leader told the researcher that "Semara Madya" started to perform *Kecak* in 1966 anticipating the tourists mainly those who would come to stay in the *Hotel Bali Beach* in Sanur, and holds a rich repertoire of the *Kecak* form of music, dance and drama forms.[1]

"Kecak Trena Jenggala" from Padang Tegal (Ubud) community started to perform *Kecak* upon the request of hotels

1. A personal interview with Ajit Dalem.

since 1973 on a contract basis, and in the temple yard as part of the *banjar* activity since 1983 on a regular basis. The culture of performing for tourists kept on expanding its sphere after three more groups from Ubud started to perform for tourists on a regular basis in the courtyard of the *Puri* Ubud from 1986. The number of groups performing for tourists in the temple and the palace yard and *banjar* building has increased dramatically in the recent years. It is estimated that performing for tourists "supports a good hundred or more troupes — two to three thousand musicians and dancers — among the 5,000 troupes listed by the provincial cultural services" (Picard 1996: 138). Since Picard wrote this, the performance culture of this nature in Ubud has expanded as several more groups perform for tourists on a regular basis. Groups formed out of women performers and university graduates have become one of the recent phenomena of the Balinese performance culture especially in Ubud.

Researchers argue that performing for tourists has become an economic adventure as it has "developed into an industry, became an organized part of the village's daily timetable, and took on a role as a major factor in the image of Ubud as a tourist destination" (Dunbar-Hall 2003: 6). Groups mostly those which perform in the *Puri* Ubud twice a week print 10,000 tickets and manage to sell them in the duration of six months. The price of ticket ranges from IR (Indonesian Rupiah) 50,000 to 80,000. Ticket sellers in streets and hotel get IR 7,000 from the sale of each ticket, and the Tourist Information Center charges IR 3,000 per ticket for printing it and advertising the performance schedule of every individual group. Groups which perform some few kilometres far from Ubud such as Junjungan have to provide a free transportation service to tourists. The price of the ticket for the show has increased across the years. During the first five months of my research most of the shows could be watched

IR 9,000 = US $1 approx.

at IR 50,000. But from 1 March 2007, four groups performing in the courtyard of the Ubud palace priced their ticket IR 80,000.

Thirty-nine groups perform for tourists in a schedule in Ubud: Ubud, Padang Tegal, Peliatan, Buntuyun and Junjungan villages located within a walking distance. Twenty-three of them perform once a week. Remaining others perform twice a week, except *Wayang Kulit* in Oka Kartini (Accommodation) that performs thrice a week. During my research, I found that there were sixty performances made in a week in Ubud. Every evening in Ubud, ticket sellers of all ages and sexes, most of them dressed in *Sarong* or traditional Balinese dress stand near the scheduled venue of the day and try to draw the attention of every passerby/tourist. Tourists coming to Ubud during the day enter the Tourists Information Centre in front of the Palace, *Puri* Ubud and gather as much information as they can. Most of the shops are closed before 7 p.m. in Ubud, and tourists are brought in or found rushing to the venue of the performance. Most of the shows begin at half past seven and last for one and a half hours except *Wayang Kulit* or Puppet Shadow theatre that begins at eight and lasts for one hour only. Twelve performances in a week are made in the courtyard of the palaces: eleven in Ubud (Water Palace Restaurant and *Puri* of (Ubud) and one in *Puri* Peliatan. Sixteen performances in a week are made in temple yard. Other performances are made in *banjar* building except *Wayang Kulit* that is performed in the hotel and private accommodation. Much also depends on nature, if it rains those performances which are supposed to take place in open place or in the courtyard of the palaces and temples are shifted to the community buildings. As it rains, some tourists even cancel their tickets because they do not want to watch the performance inside a hall or under the roof. Importantly, when temple ceremonies fall, groups belonging to that particular community cancel their performances for tourists. But tourists, expatriates and locals all gather to watch the performances made on such ceremonial occasions freely (see *fig.* 9).

Performing for tourists in Ubud may not bring such an amount of money as researchers do often think and call it an "art industry" but it has become a part of the community activities as well as hobby for local performers themselves. During my research, I saw some groups performing for a couple of audience only. I also found that in Ubud there are only few groups which can manage to draw over 50 audiences regularly during November–May, often known as "off-season" for the tourism business in Ubud. Artists who perform four days a week told the researcher that they can hardly make US $ 60 a month. Moreover, each *Kecak* group is membered by at least 150 performers, and gets 50 audiences on average. The money that the group divides, after allocating some part of it to the temple and other funds, among its members is very negligible.

Performing for Tourists: Blamed

This culture of performing for tourists is often criticized for bringing fragmentation in the formalistic structures of traditional Balinese dance, drama and musical forms. James Murdoch, an expatriate and critic on Balinese culture writes that the sponsorship provided by tourism has "reduced repertoire, which now, at the beginning of the twenty-first century, consists mostly of a small collection of the most popular works, truncated for the limited attention span — and available time — of international tourists" (2002: 7-8). Picard writes, "When one knows something of the extraordinary variety of art forms practised in Bali, one cannot help being struck by the uniformity of the tourist performances" (1996: 139). Herbest, a scholar working on the Balinese performing art and culture for over twenty-five years writes that because the distance from place to place in Bali has shrunk because of the availability of modern transportation services, "the perceptions, the personal experience of nature, which many a *dalang* and *penasar* have told me are basic to their creative process, is reduced in turn" (1997: 141). Herbest longs for the Bali untouched by the modern developments, particularly those days when performers were conditioned to leave their home at dawn to reach to the place just in time to perform. He argues that Balinese performing arts have lost the aura of the past. Traditional staging "with 270 or 360 degrees of audience seating" would create an intimate relationship between and among audience and artist, but such atmosphere has been lost these days. Audiences and performances are becoming "stationary" and "more frontal and presentational" respectively, and "group dances are replacing intricate characterization, with more elaborate, expensive costumes to catch the distanced eye" (Herbest 1997: 138). This feature of the performance culture of Bali of the present time is also criticized for creating "the endless repetition of performances" and "a deterioration in standards" and in the meantime praised as "the best groups reach high level of accomplishment, achieved through lengthy practice" (Bandem and deBoer 1995: 132-33). "[R]easons other than solely devotion" (Dibia and Ballinger 2004: 11) has been taken as the driving force behind the making of the performance culture practised for tourists in Bali, for that matter in Ubud. The practitioners of this culture are blamed for lacking a culture of respect to "the creation in its entirety" as they are found making "uncontrolled interpretation" through movements which are "mistaken" and customs which in many cases are "unlike the original conception" (Swasthi Bandem 2006: 57-58). Similarly, it is claimed that tourists in Bali come to watch "a sampling of music and dance in condensed representations"

(Dunbar-Hall 2001: 3). And, performances made for tourists are also criticized for not offering "the "scene" — the crowds, the atmosphere, the smells, sounds, and excitement of a real village or temple dance. And the experience of these is worth digging around for" (Eiseman 1996: 280).

Several factors try to bring uniformity in Ubud's performance culture. One is the historicity and importance associated with certain dance and drama forms. "Taruna Jaya," the first kind of the *Kebyar* dance created in Singaraja by Gede Manik, one of the originators of *Kebyar* music and dance, performed by a female dancer depicting a young victorious warrior, is staged for tourists by over ten performing groups. Similarly, Mario's creations have remained as the most performed pieces in the sphere of Ubud's performance culture. Over a dozen of groups perform "Kebyar Terompong" also known as "Kebyar Duduk" and "Oleg Tambullingan" also known as "Bumble Bee" dance. "Bumble Bee" was created by Mario in 1952 for "Gunung Sari" group for its world famous performances in Europe and America. Performing Mario's creation and the first *Kebyar* dance and drama pieces is regarded as presenting something authentic Balinese art not only for tourists but also for the Balinese themselves. Similarly, it is a common experience for several performing groups that tourists come, watch, go and when they come back next time, they love to watch the same dance that they had watched years back. The leader of "Panca Arta" group told the researcher that his group has been performing a particular dance-drama for a decade. His experience tells that the Japanese audience mostly those who keep on coming to Bali regularly look for his group's "Sund Upasanda" dance-drama.[2] Similarly, Putra tells that many tourists especially those who

2. A personal interview with Wayan Turun.

keep on coming to Bali and watch his group's performance may mind if he does not perform the *Baris* dance for them.[3]

The logic that performances made for tourists operate within a limited repertoire needs also be linked with the cultural and academic policies that Indonesia as a nation state and the ISI as academia have promoted and practised in Bali. The LISTIBIYA is a very influential governmental foundation that "auditions and certifies the groups for quality and authenticity (Tenzer 1991: 122), and gives a Certificate of Artistic Excellence (*Pramana Patram Budaya*) — for the groups which set to perform for tourists or go abroad to perform" (Picard 1996: 138). It performs an authority of judging the quality of the performance. Made Bandem, the former head of the ISI, defines one of the main responsibilities of the ISI as to maintain "standardness" in dance and drama forms practised for tourists or performed abroad. He holds a belief that academically trained professionals can bring refinement in the art practised and performed by locals:

> We have a responsibility at STSI to be involved in the upholding of artistic standards, particularly where tourist performances are concerned. Many groups are overworked — some perform nightly — and are not always able to do their best. We're initiating a program to have our students and graduates help to organize the village groups and negotiate on their behalf with hotel managers for reasonable performance schedules. We would also like to see some graduates employed as artistic directors at the hotels themselves, where they would organize the music and dance programs and work to educate visitors about what is presented. There are more musicians in Bali now that think of themselves as professionals in a way that was not so in the past. These artists are well positioned to play a major role in our international relations. I believe that many will be able to earn their livelihood from music before long.
>
> (Bandem in Interview with Tenzer 1991: 116-17)

3. A personal interview with A.A. Putra.

"Upholding artistic standards," a trope of academic power can also function as an agency that can bring uniformity in art forms. Moreover, art is, as Clifford Geertz argues, a topic that is "notoriously hard to talk about" not only for outsiders but also for natives and academicians, and is "beyond the reach of discourse," and "not only hard to talk about it; it seems unnecessary to do so" (1983: 94). Similarly, schools and academia of fine and performing arts are mostly found to be "dominated by the more institutionally powerful scholar/ researchers who do not know how to appraise a record of artistic accomplishment as commensurate with traditional criteria of scholarly research and publication" (Conquergood 2008: 377). As discussed in the previous chapter, Balinese dance and drama forms since the last quarter of the last century have experienced several academic inventions and interventions. Hugh writes that "Balinese performing artists are now working within an increasingly bureaucratized society dominated by tourism development. The challenge they face, along with graduates of STSI, is to maintain vitality of their heritage while building upon it to advance the arts" (1999: 256). The ISI-based artists and art teachers were asked to create some colossal form of dance dramas which are known as "super-seka" by the Seoharto-centred power zone in the past (Dibia and Ballinger 2004: 16) but such colossal dance-dramas have disappeared because they are found too difficult to be disseminated (Swasthi Bandem 2006: 55). Most of the groups performing for tourists in Ubud, as a part of hegemony, stage a couple of dance, drama and musical forms created by the ISI-based artists and art teachers. Such dance and drama forms created in academia are taken as 'standard,' thus something that is 'okayed' by academics and bureaucrats to be staged for tourists or to take them abroad.

Performing for Tourists: Defended

The following section (as well as the sixth chapter of this book mainly) aims to defy the blames made on the performances staged for the tourists in Ubud. While doing it, I try to deconstruct some of the established remarks on "touristic" performance culture in Ubud. The performance culture that has come into practice in Ubud, can be taken as an entity having "a characteristic of moving from ritual to theatre, and it has happened through participation of the audience, who pay, who come because the show is advertised, who evaluate what they are going to see before they see it" (Schechner 1983: 154). Moreover, this culture is also a part of ongoing continuity and changed state of Balinese performance culture. The *Kebyar* phenomenon, as discussed in the last chapter, brought transformations in the Balinese performance arts and cultures. It introduced several shorter forms of traditional dance and musical forms: "The forty-five minutes Legong Keraton became 15 minutes; the Kebyar Legong that was over forty-five became Taruna Jaya dance of only 15 minutes. Additionally, the thirty minutes Oleg Tumulilingan was shortened to 12 minutes" (Bandem and deBoer 1986: 9). The blame that the dance, drama and musical forms created and practised for the tourists in Ubud have become shorter and "truncated" is already deconstructed when one realizes the aestheticity and historicity associated with the *Kebyar* phenomenon in Bali and its performance culture.

As stated earlier, the *Kebyar* phenomenon brought a dynamic transformation in the Balinese performance art and culture in the first part of the last century. Picard writes that the artistic revolution of *Kebyar* detached the Balinese dance from "its theatrical content" and "ritual context" and because of this aesthetic transformation, dance became "an art form in its own right" and accessible to "spectators unfamiliar with the linguistic codes, dramaturgic conventions and literary references of the traditional dance dramas" (Picard 196: 140). McPhee writes that the *Kebyar* phenomenon brought a breakthrough as "episodes rarely reached completion, for they were continually broken off in the middle, to proceed to another tune, as though the players could not wait to begin something new" and for the dance the face of the dancer "was no longer a mask, as in the older dances, but had become mobile, human, sensitive to the slightest change in the music" (2002: 148-49). Dibia and Ballinger writes that with the advent of the *Kebyar* phenomenon the relationship of dance to music "became much more regimented" and "solo dances took precedence over dance-dramas. Today, these are the dances that visitors see in commercial venues" (2004: 52). Swasthi Bandem writes that "condensing the form by reducing the repeating movements of the traditional dance and presentation of narrative story without losing the essential of the dance" (2006: 68) has helped the traditional Balinese dance, drama and musical forms to survive in future too. The maestros who have defined dance movement organization, use of floor design, make-up, costume, stage and music in condensed form (Swasthi Bandem 2006: 68) at different aesthetic contexts of Bali can be taken as someone who were making an important attempt of wresting "tradition away from a conformism that is about to overpower it" (Walter Benjamin qtd. Wiener 1999: 51).

Some of the early *Kebyar* dance and drama forms are the most performed ones for tourists these days in Ubud. Groups performing for tourists stage up to nine dance, drama and musical forms for one and a half hour-long performance. Their performances, on the one hand, look as if they are conditioned by the pressure of tourists as audiences but, on the other hand, they evoke the historicity associated with the *Kebyar* phenomenon in the Balinese performance culture. Therefore, the *Kebyar* aesthetic revolution of the past and the culture of performing for tourists have a strong relationship as they evoke each other in the changed social and aesthetic context of Bali. Together they reveal out that the performance culture is a process in which one can find the "arguments for change, not simply for changelessness" (Valeri 1990: 155). The culture of performing both short and long, old and new, classical and modern dance, drama and musical forms for tourists is the continuation of the very aesthetic revolution that the Balinese dance, drama and music went through in the past.

Moreover, traditional performing dance and drama forms can thrive only when inventions and interventions are brought in by its practitioners. The modern version of an old art can also be made "through the intervention/invention of one or a few dedicated persons from outside the class of those they are leading" (Schechner 1983: 192). Furthermore, traditional performance culture remains alive and dynamic if it gets "evoked in the present circumstances of performance, yet, because of its ephemerality, each performance is a unique and innovative act of activity" (Lysloff 1997: 165-66). Herself a choreographer and a well-known dance teacher in Bali, Swasthi Bandem argues that traditional dances, "should not be overlooked nor should it be blindly followed." Artists in the present should make "reinterpretations and maintain levels of innovation upon its tradition" (2004: 60-61).

Performing for tourists, as Schechner terms, is a "restored behaviour." It is neither a "process of scraping away dead layers of paint to reveal the original artwork" nor a part of "unbroken tradition," but needs to be taken as the aesthetic exercises that demand "research and fieldwork" and "rehearsal in the deepest sense" (Schechner 1983: 193). John Urry writes that the performers in the dance and drama organized for tourists "become signs of what the tourist audience believes them to be. And in some cases such dancers are such powerful signifiers that the performances have become the dominant signifier of the culture in question" (2002: 156). The performances made for the tourists in Ubud are not the sign of decadence of Balinese dance and drama but markers of a prosperous performance culture, and can be linked to the logic and discourse that "the past lends authority to performance, particularly ritual performance" and "past meanings can only be conveyed in the immediacy of the present performance" (Lysloff 1997: 166). Moreover, arts flourish "when their histories are known" that's why "artists need to be able to quote and cite their antecedents, to partake of or modify or rebel against known traditions, to innovate consciously in a genre or create a new tradition knowing their works are a departure" (Erdman 1996: 292). Performers in Ubud have carved out a sphere where dissemination of Balinese dance and musical forms of all kinds, contemporary and traditional, modern and classical take place on a daily basis.

The culture of performing for tourists has made local artists more 'critical' about aestheticism associated with their art forms. In Peliatan, local artists hold a strong sense of responsibility of preserving local varieties of traditional Balinese dance and musical forms. They openly defy the domination cast by academia, for that matter the (ISI) *Indonesia Seni Institute*, the art college based in Denpasar. They put forward the logic that there is a strong need of staging and preserving local variations of traditional Balinese dance and drama forms. Peliatan had already remained as the 'capital' of art and culture for several decades in the twentieth century long before the ISI or the academia in Bali as such started to make its influence on the Balinese performing arts and culture especially from 1980s. The drama and dance forms created and practised in Peliatan represented art and culture of Bali abroad as they were staged on the occasion of the *Colonial Exhibition* in 1931 in Paris and the world famous tour of a Balinese dance group "Gunung Sari" to Europe and America in 1952. Many maestros of the Balinese dance and music worked with the Peliatan-based artists in the past. The logic of the Peliatan-based artists (discussed in the fifth chapter) reveals to us an important fact that local forms of art can also defy canonicity created by the academia from within. Since performing groups in Peliatan are formed out of the members of the *banjar* or village community, its members use the dance and drama forms that they perform for tourists as a trope of power to hold the sense of different aesthetics and identity. Performers in the Peliatan village while performing dance, drama and musical forms for tourists in the Peliatan style also perform their intellectual "self" and challenge the official discourses created by academia in Bali. As a result, tourists in Ubud and Peliatan may watch the same dance staged in different styles.

Verities Happen

The performance culture practised for the tourists in Ubud consists of multiple dance, drama and musical forms. Certain dance-drama forms are found to have comparatively lesser varieties to offer to tourists. But much also depends on whether performers are amateurs or professionals. *Barong* is regarded as a part and parcel of the *tri-hita-karana* (the Great Three Principles), typically the Balinese Hindu mode of relating 'this' with "that" world, people with gods and dead ancestors, of maintaining relationship with each other and creating a harmony within an individual soul and psyche. Zoete and Spies argue that Balinese are occupied with the nature, spirits and the magic forces which share the world with them and may considerably disturb their health and peace of mind unless their demands are satisfied (1986: 86). That is why *Barong's* outfit and mask are taken as the most sacred symbols. "Barong holds central place in offering performances" (Miettinen 1992: 132-33) in Bali. *Barong* when it walks in a procession or sits mightily in altar when offerings go on for many days holds spiritual aura. It is ritualistic, a culturally determined context or the day of performance set according to the movement of the sun and the moon makes the *Barong* performed in temple ceremonies culturally and spiritually important.

But when *Barong* is performed for tourists, it becomes an entertaining form of dance-drama. Performers act "Barong" being troubled by lice and monkey. Performing groups stage *Barong* dance in its various forms. They select a particular story and design choreography accordingly to make their "Barong" performance different. Most of the groups present "Barong Ket," also known as "Banaspati Raja" (king of the forest) but "Semara Ratih" group promises its audience to give something different. This "Barong" performed by A.A. Anom Putra assures its audience that it "dances in a focused, quiet manner, imitating natural animal movements, in contrast with the more common frenzied style" (from the Brochure of "Semara Ratih"). "Sadha Budaya" group performs "Bapang," the *Barong* dance, comparatively a very long drama based on Balinese tale of black-magic. "Sekaa Gong Sandhi Swara" group from Padang Teggal Kelod presents "Bapang" as a solo "Barong" in its usual errand followed and teased by a monkey character. "Tirta Sari" group performs "Barong Taru Pramana" based on a story in the life of the Lord Śiva. "Sekaa Gong Karyasa" group presents "Barong and Rangda Dance" as a struggle between good and evil, between *Barong*, a mythical animal that personifies good, and *Rangda*, a mythical ogre that is a personification of evil force in life and societies. Its performance also includes "Three masked men who make palm wine in the forest and attack the tiger but the tiger is helped by his monkey friend. During the fight, one man loses his nose" (Brochure). "Raja Peni Theatre" group presents "Barong Dance" based on the episode from the *Mahābhārata* epic particularly from the scene when the *Kaurava* brothers, the antagonists in the epic make a petition with the goddess Durgā to spread disease and destruction in Indraprastha, the kingdom of the five heroic *Pāṇḍava* brothers (brochure). "Panca Artha" group performs just "Barong": a ten-minute-long Barong in its usual errand, followed by a monkey character. Much also depends on the humour that the monkey character can create. The monkey character is often seen playing with the audience as it finds lice in the head of mostly lady audience, speaks in "broken" English, and shakes hands with the audience.

Similarly, several groups perform Legong dance, mostly known as "Legong Lasem" or "Legong Keraton." "Chandra Wirabhuana" and "Semara Ratih" groups perform "Legong Semardahana," a dance-drama based on a story: *Semara*, a god of love and passion, the son and *Ratih* the daughter-in-law of Śiva respectively, are asked by the divine force to disturb the age-long mediation of Śiva as a demon was found creating havoc. But the condition is that no god except Śiva could kill him. Śiva unknowingly but with a great fury emits a flame and kills his own son and daughter-in-law (brochures). "Sadha Budaya" and "Panca Artha" groups perform "Legong Lasem or Keraton" a dance drama based on a triangular love story of princess and princes. "Bina Rameja" group performs "Legong Jobog," based on the *Rāmāyaṇa* epic especially the episode where and when Rāvaṇa, the king of demon disguised as Mārīca or deer arrives to fool Rāma, Sītā and Lakṣmaṇa, and ends at the point when Rāma and Sītā meet. But the role of Hanumān becomes prominent in the performance of "Bina Rameja" as it is Hanumān who defeats Rāvaṇa not Rāma. "Tirta Sari," "Genta Bhuana Sari," "Gunung Sari," "Sekaa Gong Werdha Arma," "The Peliatan Masters," the Peliatan village-based groups present "Legong Keraton," a dance-drama that was created and circulated in Peliatan in the first half of the twentieth century. "Panca Artha" group performs "Legong Trance," a dance-drama that shows singing Surgawi, two beautiful dancers (*Legong*) who "start dancing with lithe and delicate movement in trance." This dance is based on the story in which gods give mercy and blessing for peace and prosperity of humans (brochure). "Tirta Sari" group performs "Legong Jobog," a dance-drama based on the story of two brothers, Bāli and Sugrīva, the characters from the epic *Rāmāyaṇa* and their fights. "Chandra Virbhuvan" also performs "Legong Abhimanyu," (see *fig.* 10) a dance and drama based on the life of Abhimanyu, son of Arjuna from the epic *Mahābhārata* and was created in 1982 by I. Wayan Dibia (dance) and I. Ketut Tama (music) (brochure). "Yama Sari" group performs "Legong Kuntir" based on the story of two brothers who contend over the water which gives them eternal lives. "Theatre Raja Peni" group presents "Legong Kuntul" that dramatises the playfulness of a pair of birds in the rice field (brochure). "Sekaa Gong Jaya Swara" group presents "The Legong Superba Duta of *Mahābhārata* Epic" and is performed by five ladies. The five dancers are the *apsaras*es (nymphs) sent by Indra to disturb the meditation of the demon *Newatakwaca* brothers just in time before they could shake the heaven through the power they were going to acquire (brochure). "Panca Artha" and "Sekaa Gong Sandhi Swara" groups perform one hour long dance-drama "Sunda Upasunda: A Story from the *Mahābhārata* in the Legong Style," and is about two demon brothers: Sunda and Upasunda who wish to possess the power to rule the universe but were destroyed by the *apasaras*es or nymphs sent by Indra (brochure).

Unlike "Barong" and "Legong," the "Baris" though has its variations, only a few of its forms are performed for tourists in Ubud. A solo *Baris* dance known as "Baris Tunggal" developed from strictly religious dance to an enthralling solo performance depicting the different moods of young heroic warrior is the most performed *Baris* dance for tourists in Ubud. "Sekaa Gong Jaya Swara" and "Mekar Sari" groups perform a group "Baris" dance. Moreover, most of the groups have young *Baris* dancers and as a result their dance takes a faster pace of movement. A.A. Putra, "a Bali famous Baris dancer" (from brochure) tells that young dancers find it very difficult to evoke and articulate the fear and courage that *Baris* lives and goes through: "It is not the completion of the Baris dance that is important, but the very process of creating some moments of being a 'real' warrior based on 'the Baris world' that is important."[4]

Similarly, Balinese mask dance that depicts an eternal battle between vice and virtue too has got its variations. But "Jauk Manis" is found to be the most performed mask dance in Ubud. Other mask dances performed for tourists include "Telek," and "Topeng Tua." "Topeng," though traditionally performed by all men, "Luh Luwih Women's gamelan group" broke the tradition by having women in all the roles (brochure). Moreover, individual talents have created new dance and drama forms out of the traditional Balinese mask dance repertoire in the recent times. "Kan Cing Wie" is a recent creation based on the heritage of Balinese mask dance created by Jimat, "someone who can combine tourist success with a traditional role" (Vickers 1989: 207), and is being performed by a group called "Topeng Jimat" in the stage of the Arma Museum once a week. This one-hour-long drama tells about a king's

4. Ibid.

adventure into the world of supernatural:

> Two comic servants, Pensars wearing a half mask tell the audience that their King Jayapangus intends to survey the world outside. Two Legong Dedari appear as "queens" making a quarrel over the King. A performer wearing a mask of Topeng Sidakarya, mother of one the queens comes forward in her fury and through her curse transforms the king and the other queen into Jero Gede and Jero Luh, the male and female giant puppets named Barong Landung. This transformation of Jayapangus and his Chinese mistress Kang Cing Wi is bestowed with magic power and required to guard and protect villages and villagers from demonic influences, and thus they need to be honoured as magical scared effigies. (Brochure)

This new creation of Jimat, the world famous Balinese "Topeng dancer" can be taken as an example of how individual talents in Bali have been working with the heritage of the Balinese performing art and culture, and have managed to create something new that goes along with faith and beliefs of the Balinese.

The next thing that has helped to bring varieties in Ubud's performance culture is the pressure created by tourists from Japan in the recent years. Japan has remained as the largest number of tourists-coming-nation to Bali since 2001. This has started to cast some influences in the very performance culture in Ubud (see *fig.* 11). Japanese entrepreneurs and lovers of Balinese art and culture have become recent patrons of several performing groups in Ubud. "Yamasari" group and the venue that this group performs once a week was formed and built with the economic and moral support from a Japanese scholar. Two "Bamboo Gamelan" groups perform for tourists in Ubud. "Bamboo Gamelan" is a very popular form of art in Negara, northern part of Bali, some 25 km away from Ubud. But it is being performed in Ubud with the purpose of catering mainly to the taste of the Japanese audience for the last few years. This has become possible through the help of a Japanese entrepreneur who runs hotel business in Ubud, and is known as Wayan Suzuki.

Performing in a Different Manner

Several contemporary dance and drama forms created by the ISI-based artists are also performed regularly in Ubud. The number of groups formed, led and membered by the ISI graduates has increased in the recent years. The ISI graduates and graduating artists are more conscious of mentioning the name of the composer and the choreographer of music and dances that they perform for tourists. Groups formed and led by the ISI graduates have young members and perform some new creations along with classical and *Kebyar* form of dance, music and drama to tourists. "Semera Ratih," "Nirtta Dewi," and "Spirit of Bali" groups led and membered by the ISI graduates hold a richer repertoire of contemporary creations. However, groups like "Tirta Sari," "Gunung Sari" and "Yamasari," all from the Peliatan village defy the ISI influence, and offer a rich repertoire of dance and drama in the local styles. Several groups present new creations of their own. "Semera Ratih" presents a musical creation of its own that promises to give "an exciting new selection of pieces including Kecak, a combination of instrumental and vocal" (brochure). "Sekaa Gong Jaya Swara" starts its performance with a procession to the stage from the temple located nearby giving an impression of a cultural celebration. Groups such as "Tirta Sari," "Gunung Sari," "Anang Sari," "Yamasari" and "Nirtta Dewi" perform their own creations. "Tirta Sari" presents instrumental "Sekar Gendot" that adapts music played by four genders that accompany the Wayang Kulit (Puppet Theatre). This group too has its own instrumental and dance creations. "Yamasari" group presents "Segara Muncar" or "Ujan Mas," a musical interpretation of the feeling expressed by rain. It was composed by Hendrawan, the leader of this group, in 1997. This group also performs "Puspa Raga," its own creation made for its Japan visit in 1996. "Chandra Wirabhuana" has its instrumental piece called "Cerukcuk Wana" that depicts the world of Cerukcuk birds: "The unusual sound results from the combination of pentatonic and septatonic pelog scales (or moods) first heard in Balinese music in the mid-1980s" (brochure). "Cerukcuk Punyah," an instrumental composed for "Chandra Wati Ladies Gamelan Group," is an "expression of heartfelt joy communicated in the form of melody and rhythm" (brochure). "Genta Bhuana Sari" and "Sekaa Gong Werdha Arma" present songs and instrumental called "Kebyar Susun" created in 1966 by Wayan Gandra who used to perform in Peliatan in the past (brochure). "Panca Arta" presents "Lencana Agung Ubud" that promises to paint a picture of life in Ubud. Symbols and banners holding *Ardha Candra* (half moon), windhu (*śūnya*, the void), *nāga* (the king Cobra) and macro-cosmos carried out by performers are meant to represent life and soul in their harmonious world. "The spirit and vibrant energy described by the symbols, convinces the viewer that the society of Ubud has been given a gift of special and natural depth" (brochure).

Similarly, "Nirtta Dewi" group promises to present at least one new musical and dance creation for tourists every week. Kadek Dewi, herself a graduate from the ISI and a famous "Taruna Jaya" dancer told the researcher that her group aims to bring classical, modern and contemporary creations together. This group performs "Tabuh Nyeraki (2005)," an instrumental piece that uses Western instruments and incorporates traditional Balinese gamelan interlocking patterns, and is composed by I. Made Subandi, S. Sn. (brochure). This group also performs "Dara Dewi" that illustrates the majestic grandeur of goddess of heaven and is choreographed by Kadek Dewi herself and composed by Agus Teja Sentosa, S. Sn. (brochure). "Semara Ratih" presents "Instrumental Gadung Melati," a new welcome dance that uses elements of "Legong" and "Rejang," created by Dr I. Wayan Dibia in 2003 (brochure). This welcome dance looks more secular and contemporary than the Peliatan-styled welcome dance that mostly holds religious and spiritual movements and expressions. "Sekaa Gong Anangga Sari" group performs an instrumental "Sekar Sari": a piece composed in 1999 by I. Ketut Cater. "Spirit of Bali" group presents an instrumental "Lekesan" composed by I. Nyoman Windha by using different Indonesian musical traditions created for the 2001 "Bali Arts Festival" to evoke diversity of Indonesian art and culture (brochure). "Seka Gong Jaya Swara" group performs two creations of Wayan Sudirana: an instrumental called "Bituka" and dance known as "Tedung Agung Dance" performed by male and female dancers to welcome guests (brochure).

"Manuk Rawa," created by Dibia that depicts a flock of water birds, "Kijang Kencana (Shining Deer)," composed by I Gusti Agung Nugrah Supartha in 1983 that depicts the cheerful life of a herd of deer in the forest, "Tari Belbis" that portrays the behaviour of a flock of wild ducks in their natural surroundings, "Candrawasih,"(see *fig.* 12) choreographed by Ni Luh Swasthi Wijaya in 1988 that depicts the courtship of two Birds of Paradise, "Tari Kelinci" (Rabbit Dance) by Nyoman Carita from the ISI that depicts the world of fun that the Rabbits live with, "Gopala Dance" a creation inspired by the artists of Bali that celebrates the rice harvest, "Mekepung" that depicts a water buffalo race, and "Kupu-Kupu Tarum" that depicts dance of butterflies of heaven — are some other new creations of the ISI and the ISI-based artists and teachers.

These dances also reflect the contemporary trend of the Balinese dance, drama and musical forms. They evoke the world of birds and animals, and are also the pieces performed regularly for the tourists in Ubud.

Most of the groups arrange their dance and drama into an order of: three classical, three Kebyar and two new creations. Ms Aryani, the leader of "Nirtta Dewi" group says that tourists understand nuances of new creations better than locals. She believes that several contemporary dance and drama creations in Bali are abstract and many also complain about it. She argues that for the last five years most of the Balinese dance forms have given up the story, and this should not be taken as the decadence of Balinese performing arts. She as a university graduate wants to explore new forms and argues that one should not harp on the belief that dance and drama in abstract form and spirit lack some beauty and energy. "Tourists, naturally, prefer classical Balinese dance and drama forms. But to limit oneself to the classical forms because they are loved by tourists is to stop himself/herself from learning and practising new forms of art." And, most of the new creations that Aryani and her group members have created borrow or are based on the classical form and style (see *fig.* 13). "They are not brought from the West, but come from the repertoire of the tradition-based movement and style. Many groups perform only classical dance and music because they lack man-power that can create new pieces out of the vocabulary and idioms of the classical dance and drama forms,"[5] says Aryani.

Moreover, Putra, the leader of "Semara Ratih" group says that even the old narrative dance and dramas regarded as classical do become abstract if the performer cannot feel and concentrate in form that one watches in Ubud or elsewhere. He further argues that many performers of the classical

5. A personal interview with Kadek Dewi Aryani.

Balinese dance and drama do sometimes unnecessarily get into fast tempo, and thus miss the art of concentration and quality of creating moods. It is not finishing the dance *per se* but the very art or process of creating it that audience both tourists and locals love to watch. "Anything that does not come with feeling and concentration is not piece of art. The "inner eyes" have to see the dangerous animal before the Baris dancer performer lets his or her gestures create the very moment. Gestures created with sudden and without enough emotion can kill the beauty of the art and aesthetics of the classical Balinese dance and drama. Abstract is not only related with contemporary art,"[6] argues Putra.

Kecak Means Kecaks

Kecak performed for tourists is mostly regarded as a single form of art, and is often associated with the joint-creative effort of the Balinese local artists of Bedulu village and a German musician, Walter Spies. It is also taken as a "prerequisite of cultural tourism" as it has "strong connections with artistic developments in the creation of works for tourist consumption" (Dunbar-Hall 2001: 6-7). Spies, the important man behind the invention of a particular form of *Kecak* writes that *Kecak* was developed through a rehearsal of "the utmost precision to the last detail, literally for months on end" and has lost nothing of the ecstatic ritual character which it had as an accompaniment of the trance-dance Sanghynag" (1986: 83). Dibia, a choreographer, researcher and teacher of *Kecak* dance drama writes that the secular *Kecak* though was first created in Bedulu, Gianyar through the joint efforts of the German-born artist Walter Spies and the people of Bedulu under the leadership of Limbak, it is the people of Bona who had a major role in the development of dramatic *Kecak* as they refined the formal

6. A personal interview with A.A. Putra.

structure of *Kecak* and established the standard scene for "The Abduction of Sītā" (2000: 8).

Individual *Kecak* performance in Ubud employs various aesthetic tools and skills as part of maintaining its difference (see *fig*. 14). All *Kecak* performances staged in Ubud for tourists are based on the *Rāmāyaṇa* epic, but each of them aims at presenting the story thus carving out visualities differently. Almost all *Kecak* groups give brief information to history and aesthetics of the *Kecak* dance-drama before they perform it for tourists. Their brochures reveal that they want to highlight sound and visual semiotics of *Kecak*. "Choir of more than one hundred men who sit in a concentric circle and sing, sway, stand and lying prone," "voices and dances tell the unfolding tale" and "multi-layered sounds of cak cak cak" are some of the phrases used by the groups in their brochures. There are eight *Kecak* groups in Ubud, and their brochures heavily borrow words and expressions from the academic write-ups especially by Clune and Stephensen, Spies and Zoete, and Wayan Dibia.

Kecak presented by "Sekaa Kecak Padang Subadra," "Desa Adat Sambahan," "Taman Kaja," "Trena Jenggala," "Krama Desa Adat Junjugan" and "Sekaa Kecak "Sandhi Suara" has almost the same plot. The story begins and ends in a linear order. It starts with the arrival of Mārīca, a beautiful but a disguised deer form of Rāvaṇa, the demon king at a time when Rāma and Sītā are making love. It ends when Sugrīva manages to kill Meghanāda, the son of Rāvaṇa. Though the story and plot matches, the presentation of each group differs in terms of choreography. Either Hanumān or Rāma or Sugrīva, either of the protagonist characters from the epic dominates the performance of one or the other group. Then there are clowns, *pensar* who "go back and forth between the various characters of the classical past," and "enjoy considerable liberty of expression, interpreting the words and manners of their masters through parody and presenting a double grotesque of them" (Picard 1996: 144), and add new flavours in individual *Kecak* performance.

Choreographers have played important roles in creating diverse forms of sound and visualities of *Kecak*. Spectacular scenes such as those which aim to visualise or evoke the episode of war from the epic make the individual *Kecak* performance different and unique. "Krama Desa Adat Junjugan Kecak" group acts out the magical arrow of Meghanāda that binds Rāma and Lakṣmaṇa very naturalistically as a green and 10 m long mask of a dragon is performed by over ten performers (see *fig.* 15). When Garuḍa, the majestic bird breaks the spell of this magical spear of Meghanāda, the green giant dragon is seen making an exit from the stage. In the same performance, there is a scene where Kumbhakarṇa, brother of Rāvaṇa is brought into the battlefield by over a dozen of *Kecak* players and is again taken out after he is killed. These visual semiotics make the *Kecak* performance of the group from Junjugan village strikingly spectacular and different.

Kecak by "Krama Desa Ubud Kaja" group is subtitled with "The Death of Kumbhakarṇa." It is the very scene where Kumbhakarṇa, the brother of Rāvaṇa goes to fight with Rāma and Lakṣmaṇa reluctantly that comes into prominence. Finally, Kumbhakarṇa dies. But Rāma sends Kumbhakarṇa's soul to heaven. The performance ends with a moral message. This conditions the visual structure of the *Kecak* performance that this group stages. "Semara Madya Kecak" group from the Peliatan village presents only an hour long *Kecak* performance. Sound and choreography — thus the speed of dense visualities — makes the performance of this group different. Almost all *Kecak* groups except "Semara Madya" from Peliatan perform the fire dance followed by the *Rāmāyaṇa*-based dance-drama. Mostly, the fire dancers come from the Bono village. *Kecak* by both "Trena Jenggala" and "Sekaa Kecak Sandhi Suara" groups from Padang Tegal have three pieces: *Kecak* performance which are comparatively faster in their visual narrative, "Sanghyang Dedari Dance," the essential religious dance that is believed to possess a divine power to maintain health and well-being of the village, and finally a fire dance.

Dibia writes that the vocal chants in *Kecak* are of two types: regular, adapted from the more contemporary melodic lines of gong *Kebyar*, and irregular, taken from the ancient *Sanghyang* trance. And they serve two primary functions: interlude between scenes, and accompany the scene and support the dramatic narrative, and together they establish the dramatic mood (2000: 11-20). Such formalistic features of *Kecak* have allowed artists to create or invent newer elements to mark the distinctness of an individual group's performance. Major stylistic innovations in the formalistic features of *Kecak* dance-drama appeared in the 1960s and 1970s. Senior *Kecak* performers told the researcher that the *Kecak* performances of the past were visually simple. Dibia writes that *Kecak* performances in the past were presented in a more loosely organised story. They also employed fewer, simpler, rhythmic patterns and sustained a slower tempo and featured a significant amount of irregular chanting in conjunction with other expressive and mysterious sounds. But contemporary *Kecaks* now have got much more complex and faster tempo, and the chorus has got shorter roles (2000: 54-55). This phenomenon undergone by *Kecak* as a form of art in Bali can be linked with the logic put by Schechner that historical changes make even the exact replication of the original form of art even different than the original event (1983: 71).

The quality of *Kecak* performance, as I. Nyoman Martajya told the researcher, is determined by the mood of performers. Even a single fresh voice can bring energy of a different scale in the performance. One performer can bring new energies in others. *Kecak* like any other kind of performance is also dependent on the mind and feeling of the performers. It is believed that the physique of performers also matters, the healthier and stronger the performers, the more powerful will be his or her voice. That is why many *Kecak* group leaders want youths from their *banjar* and village take part in the *Kecak* performance staged for tourists. Such participation of youths, Nyoman believes, will help youths to socialise themselves as well as to secure a future for performance culture in Ubud.[7] Finally, *Kecak* as one of the most popular art forms among tourists in Bali is a living and vibrant form of art. This has become possible because individual performing groups look for innovation, and get engaged within the repertoire of art and skill of making of *Kecak* performance in newer styles. The culture of performing *Kecak* for tourists over the last five decades has created an intangible but a significant "flow" of art and knowledge of staging it in diverse forms.

Changes but Slow

Several factors make performance culture in Ubud change slowly as each group needs to carve out its niche. Several groups perform once a week. They mostly perform the same dance, drama and musical forms which they have been practising for years with occasional improvisations. They cannot make drastic changes in their presentation because of social, aesthetic and formalistic factors of their performances. When a *banjar* decides to form a *Kecak* group, a member from every household is expected to join the several-month-long rehearsal. Mostly, a *Kecak* group has at least 150 members in it. A several months-long rehearsal for such a group, made of heterogeneous members — farmers, students, shop owners and housewives among others — is a mega adventure that is possible once a decade only. There can be some minor

7. A personal interview with I. Nyoman Martajya.

adjustments in individual performance, but the plot and choreography cannot be changed overnight, say most of the *Kecak* group leaders. That's why so much depends on choreography which can make performance of individual *Kecak* group different.

It is not only the *Rāmāyaṇa*-based *Kecak* performances but also dance dramas presented in Legong and Barong styles do not change overnight. "Panca Arta" group has not changed its dance drama "Sunda-Upasanda." This group mostly presents the classical Balinese dance and drama forms. The leader told me that their dance and drama are loved by tourists and are performed for temple ceremonies, and thus loved by locals too. "Theatre Raja Peni" stages almost one hour-long dance drama based on the *Mahābhārata* that employs "Barong" and "Rangda" dance. Changing plot in the performance means starting things from the very beginning again.

Some Needed Transformations

Two "Wayang Kulit" or Puppet Theatre groups in Ubud perform at eight in the evening for one hour only. The performance takes place inside a non-descript room. The group from the Monkey Forest area performs at *Kertha Accommodation* in the house owned by I. Made Gender, himself a puppet master and who also performs for other *Legong* and *Barong* groups as well. This group performs two pieces: a drama based on the epic *Mahābhārata* and another short drama based "The Gripping Tale of Black Magic: Calona-rang." Other group performs at Oka Kartini hotel, in a room and performs drama based on the *Mahābhārata* and the *Rāmāyaṇa*.

In "Wayang Kulit" performance, the *Dalang* or the puppeteer works as the leader and is paid higher than the musicians involved. Since "Wayang Kulit" draws lesser number of tourists, the system of dividing money among group members and venues runs in a "flexible" system. In "high-season" of tourism, the house owner in the Monkey Forest area takes 80 per cent of the total income. But in "low season" he does not charge any money for the venue. The owner gives space, instruments tools and everything required to perform "Wayang Kulit." Musicians and *Dalang* come and perform and divide money among group members.[8] Since there are only few performers, from six to twelve in a "Wayang Kulit" group, it keeps group members financially safe even though it gets comparatively lesser number of audiences.

Performance of "Wayang Kulit" is essentially required for every rite of passage that the Balinese need to go through. But cultural importance attached with "Wayang Kulit" alone cannot draw the audience especially tourists to the venue. A *Dalang* who can recount "tales spanning centuries and continents" and improvize "complex tapestry of court intrigues, great loves, great wars, deep philosophy, magic, mysticism, and at brilliantly conceived moments, comedy" (Ness and Prawirohardjo 1985: 1) as he holds strings and sings may not help to bring a flow of tourists to the venue either. Since "Wayang Kulit" is performed on different cultural occasions at different places, Balinese can watch it in the inner part of the temple, in the *banjar* building and in their home. But when it is performed for tourists, tourists find themselves crammed into a little room. "Wayang Kulit" needs a dark room for it to be articulated into visualities that audience can easily see, enjoy and understand but such venues too can be created and given a better transformation, leaders of performing groups in Ubud argue. I. Made Winastara who makes puppet shadow performance in his own house in Jalan Gautama lane on the request of tourists is not happy with the venue though he makes performances only a few times a year.

8. A personal interview with I. Ketut Pasek and I. Made Gender.

Thus performing for tourists is not a mere act of presenting dance and drama readily available from their storehouse. Forces that try to bring uniformity in performances made for tourists are counter-balanced by forces that aim at creating varieties within. Performing for tourists can also create a competitive zone where artists vie to carve out spaces through innovative works. It can enable artists to experience the very continuity and change state of their performance culture in a pragmatic manner as they set to create new forms as well as stage traditional forms in local variations. Importantly, this enables artists to create an important zone of invention and dissemination of old and new forms of art, and redefine sacredness and secularity associated with dance and drama forms, and make practitioners more vigilant about their culture and art forms. Thus performing for tourists is more than performing for tourists which is the subject of the next chapter.

5

Past, Present and Future of the Culture of Performing for Tourists in Ubud

Tourism and Ubudians

THE nexus between local performance culture and tourism business is a subject of serious discussion. It is argued that local culture and tourism both can be invented and intensified, and tourism is "part of a reflexive process where all the actors learn from experiences," and tourism industry "adapts and develops, tourists respond with changing tastes and preferences, and locals rework their identities and strategies in changing conditions" (Crang 2004: 75). Tourism does not come alone but brings in roles and awareness of diverse ranges — from economic to spiritual — for its participants involved in the making of a specific cultural site for it. Things such as local heritage, sustainable culture and environment become subjects of creations and concerns as they go through a process of reinterpretation "to address new grounds through which tourism generates significance and value" (Crouch 2004: 94). Tourism stimulates even "ethically driven entrepreneurs" to explore "entrepreneurial culture which is associated with the shifting consumption patterns of postmodernism" (Shaw 2004: 131), and defines the spatial location of tourism activity as "an inherent aspect of the product" (Ashworth 2004: 211). To locals, it sets roles to define, intensify and extend their cultures as part of "an exercise in accentuating the local uniqueness of a destination site" (Chang 2004: 223).

Moreover, tourism offers locals not only opportunities to run business but also a situation where their ability "to interpret their own cultures, to defend the integrity of their cultures, and to receive compensation for the use and enjoyment of their cultural manifestations by tourists becomes increasingly challenged" (d'Hauteserre 2004: 241). Local culture in the context of tourism business is not only an entity that remains as the object of "commodification" but can also experience the state of "cultural evolution" and "question of authenticity" (Hinch 2004: 250). When tourists start to "see and represent" locals and their daily environment, locals too keep on "constructing and constituting the way" to see their own "environment, other places, cultures, and nature" (Saarinen 2004: 446). As a result, the issue of consumption of local culture by visitors or tourists becomes as much important as its consumption by host or locals (Ateljevic 2004: 295). Finally, agencies of tourism business too determine its nature and scope as they create "a whole industrial network of image makers overseas" and influence many Third World countries' "tourism on our terms" policy (Crick 2004: 325-26).

As discussed in the earlier chapters, the researchers, locals, tourists, the Indonesian cultural and tourism policy makers, and tourism business runners of national and international order have helped the Ubudians to carve out a performance culture that they could offer to their tourists, gods and themselves at the present times. Ubud like other villages in Bali had had its local performance culture of a certain magnitude but once it became a tourist destination, the Ubudians set out to invent and intensify their local performance culture not only for tourists but also for themselves. Ubud now has become a geo-cultural space within

Bali where not only tourists but also locals encounter a performance culture of a greater magnitude.

The Past and the Present of Performing for Tourists in Ubud

Several artistic and societal factors have played important roles in the making of the Ubud's performance culture. First, there is a noble history and heritage of dance, musical and drama forms created in new forms in Peliatan. The Peliatan village since the 1920s has remained as an important centre for learning and practising newer creations in Bali. Several world famous modern Balinese dance and musical forms were created for the first time in Peliatan, and they are known for holding the Peliatan aesthetics now. In the 1930s, McPhee wrote about the performance of the Peliatan-based group "Gunung Sari" in the following manner: "I had always found their playing rather impersonal. It had a cold brilliance that was spectacular but not moving. But their technique was perfection, and they played the latest, *Kebyar* pieces, learned directly from the foremost composers of North Bali" (2002: 148). "Gunung Sari" was the group that performed for the first time outside Bali. Many maestros of the Balinese dance and music in the past including Mario would come and practise their new creations for this group. For example, "Bumble Bee" dance was invented by Mario for "Gunung Sari" for its tour to Europe and America in 1952. Therefore, artists in Peliatan had already carved out a long history of performing for tourists inside Bali and abroad before they set out to perform for tourists on a regular basis in their village (see *fig.* 16).

Agung Mandera (1905-81) (see *fig.* 17) is a name of pride for performers of all ages and sexes in Peliatan. Agung was a musician and a dancer who performed in both the world famous tours of "Gunung Sari" mentioned above. Musicians and dancers from Sanur, Peliatan and Sayang took part in those tours. Sukawati, the prince and king of the *Puri* Ubud was the only man from Ubud, and he was not a dancer but a tour manager who knew how to market art.[1] Great dancers of Bali of the 1920s, the 1930s and of the later decades of the last century worked with Mandera. Sons, daughters, friends and disciples of late Mandera lead groups which perform for tourists in Peliatan, and they prefer to stage dances in the Peliatan style, and enthusiastically make the discourse of the Peliatan kind of Balinese aesthetics. The former President of Indonesia, Soekarno would call Mandera, the then leader of "Gunung Sari" to create new dances with the purpose of staging for his international guests. "Helicopter sent by the President would pick Mandera up from Peliatan and would take to the Palace in Tampaksiring. Mandera would be asked to create a new dance for the guests coming for yet another international event," recalls Hendrawan, the present leader of the group. And, this was how and when "Legong" dance that the tourists and the Balinese watch these days got condensed in its form. It was also the time when Peliatan became a centre for learning some excellent Balinese dance and musical forms. Mandera was one of the main minds that carved out spaces for the Peliatan style dance and drama forms.

"Sadha Budaya," a group of the musicians and dancers from Ubud, formed in the early 1980s, was the first such effort to bring new confidence among the villagers in Ubud. A group made from all of the then twelve but now thirteen *banjar*s of Ubud reawakened "the spirit of music making throughout the village and in no time one could see excitement was "building and the temples were packed for ceremonies. This made me — and all of Ubud — very happy" (Rai in interview

1. A personal interview with Hendrawan.

with Tenzer 1991: 118-19). By the end of 2008, over a dozen groups perform in the Ubud village, and six groups perform in Peliatan.

The native impulse "to create and experiment" and remain "very critical of the production of every other" (1986: 44-45) that Zoete and Spies noticed about Balinese in the first quarter of the twentieth century has not only given to a rich repertoire of dance, drama and musical forms and styles but has also increased the very repertoire of the art and the skills of managing the performance culture in Bali at the present times. Balinese performance cultures, researchers argue, have gone through major process of transformation at present times especially after tourism has become the major mode of earning for Balinese. Balinese performing artists have become more mobile, and the gamelan set which was once very difficult to be owned by the "gentry" class (Tenzer 1991: 75) is owned by community-based clubs and groups now. Village communities in Bali do no longer hold competitions among their performing groups on a regular basis. But they send troupes of both sexes and all ages formed out of the members of the village or *deśa* to take part in the *Bali Art Festival*. Thereby, the group earns name and fame locally as well as nationally, and gives a continuation to the same heritage of the performance culture that Spies and his fellow researchers and travellers experienced in Bali in those days in the 1920s and 1930s but in a newer context. Several groups performing for tourists mention the achievements that they have made by performing abroad and winning medals in different art competitions and festivals held in Bali and Indonesia in their brochures to assert their identity to their audience. "The Spirit of Bali" regards itself as a "number one group" of Bali since it has won several awards in the *Bali Art Festival*. It performs at Pura Desa Kutuh every Tuesday and charges its audience some "extra" money for taking picture and recording its performance, and does also promise to offer different programmes every week.

Groups performing for tourists in Ubud do not hold the same historicity. Most of the groups were formed in the 1980s. There are half a dozen groups formed recently. During my research, I watched two new groups making their debut performance. I also watched an extensive rehearsal process that a *Women's Gamelan* group was going through before it would finally be permitted to perform for tourists. On the other hand, "Gunung Sari" has already made a nine-decade long history of performing for tourists. This group possesses history, heritage and pride of an important order for the Balinese artists.

Leaders of many historically important groups do share a common experience that performing for tourists in the past was not that easy. When "Tirta Sari" from Peliatan started to perform for tourists, the job of marketing its business came as a great challenge to the group. The group leader, Dalem, the son of Mandera, told the researcher that he and his friends would go to Kuta and Sanur and distribute brochures among tourists and travel agents then. Luckily tourists would arrive on the day mentioned in the brochure. "Kecak Trena Jenggala," now led by I. Ketut Sandi, was formed in 1953 but started to perform for tourists since 1973 on a contract basis mainly in hotels located in the *Puri* Ubud and Campuan Hotels, all run and managed by the members of the *Puri* Ubud. Finally, it started to perform at Padang Tegal in its own community temple on a regular basis since 1983. This group is regarded as one of the oldest *Kecak* groups in Ubud.

Putu Suadini, the leader of "Women's Janger" group and "Chandrawati Gamelan group" told the researcher that she along with her friends would dress up in late afternoon and walk up to the hotel yard to perform for tourists in the late 1970s. Performing at hotel yard in the beginning was an exciting experience since they would get to "watch swimming pool and tourists." "Mostly, it would be night by the time tourists would gather, and despite mosquito bites we would wait and perform and return home late at night,"[2] recalls Ms. Suadini.

Desak Nyoman Suarti, now a famous female entrepreneur of Bali remembers the time when she along with her friends used to go to the *Hotel Bali Beach* to perform for tourists. She narrates:

> Walking in the marbled Hotel lobby itself was a great psychological adventure for me and my friends. We would look at our own bare feet and felt a kind of hesitation. And after the show, performers were allowed to take buffet dinner and that too would make us more confused as we did not know what to do with spoon and fork. I and my fellow group members would hire a truck and load all instruments, put on make up and would reach the hotel by late afternoon. Sometimes it would rain on the way. Performing for tourists then was not taken as a life long profession. Most of us were not serious about performing for tourists then.[3]

Only when tourists in million started to arrive in Bali from 1980s, artists started dreaming of surviving on the profession of performing for tourists. There would be so many performances for tourists in Ubud, it was never realized then.

Professional dancers and musicians and academicians from Ubud narrate a common experience of how difficult was it to form a group in the early 1980s. Individual musicians and dancers from the then twelve but now thirteen *banjar*s from Ubud were selected to form a performing group named

---

2. A personal interview with Putu Sudani.
3. An interview with Desak Nyoman Suarti.

"Sada Budaya." Swastika, a music instructor and *guru* of several women gamelan groups and Prof. Rai, the former rector of the ISI told the researcher that they had had a very hard time in convincing local leaders and musicians about the importance of forming a group based on multi-*banjars*. Once the group got formed and started to perform at ceremonies and for tourists, the quality of the performances in Ubud started to go up. And "Bina Remaja," "Panca Arta" and "Jaya Swara" groups formed in the latter years of the 1980s helped to intensify the performance culture practised for tourists in Ubud. Swastika Raka told the researcher that it was very difficult to practise and carry out rehearsal in the past. It would be hard to make all group members gather for rehearsals but things have changed for good as everyone holds a mobile phone these days, and as an instructor he is in contact with them, and improvization in performances can be made in time.

Banjar and Ubud's Performance Culture

In the remaining part of this chapter, I argue that the culture of performing dance, drama and musical forms for tourists has enabled locals in Ubud to perform their ages-old art, skill and tradition of managing performing groups, community activities, ceremonies and rituals together in a newer social context. This culture has enabled them to get engaged within the history and heritage of the traditional Balinese performing art and culture, and give the latter a vibrant continuation. Groups performing for tourists in Ubud can be divided into two: *banjar* and non-*banjar* or village communities in terms of their organizational structure. Groups formed out of a single-*banjar* member dominate the performance culture in Ubud though the number of groups formed out of the non-*banjar* members has increased in the recent years. However, such categories are not rigid as most of the performers perform for both types of groups, and groups of both natures hold equal historicity and importance in the making of the Ubudian performance culture. Since a single *banjar*-based group cannot necessarily have all the professionals required for the performances made for tourists, some dancers and musicians are always hired by one or the other group. This necessity brings in professionals from different communities and *banjar*s together in a single forum, and creates a cross-*banjar* flow of art and skill of dance and musical styles. Since several performing groups in Ubud are formed out of the members belonging to a single *banjar*, the *banjar*-based groups collect a fund out of the money that they manage to make by performing for tourists. The fund is used for managing rituals and ceremonial performances in temple, and importantly, for teaching traditional and modern Balinese dance, drama and musical forms to local children and women. Heads of many performing groups in Ubud are also the leaders of the respective *deśa* and *banjar*. The particular evening of the performance for tourists becomes an occasion of meeting, or for that matter, performing social and communal relationship for the villagers. This meeting enables them to arrange some minutes to discuss and solve several issues from irrigation to cremation.

The mega-tourism project in Bali in the 1970s, as discussed in the earlier chapter, offered the *adat* and the *banjar*, the ages-old Balinese traditional and cultural village organizations a responsibility to create awareness among locals about the importance of intensifying festivals, ceremonies and dances to draw a bigger flow of tourists to their villages. Once *banjar*s decided to form groups to perform for tourists, the custodians of the performance culture set out to work with their age-old skills and wisdom of managing performing groups. And while doing so they have reiterated the very zeal of creating dance and music in newer styles that the Balinese are so much praised for. Since the heads who lead the *deśa* and *banjar* are primarily responsible for maintaining ceremonies, for that matter, organizing dance and drama in village temples, forming groups to perform for tourists became one more but important activity of the entire community. Since as a matter of cultural need every *banjar* needs to own resources such as performers, gamelan orchestra, costumes and masks needed for conducting ceremonies of one or the other kind, performing for tourists has become an extension of the same matrix of the performance culture that the *banjar* and its members have nurtured for millennia (see *fig.* 18). The amount of money that a group manages to save in its community fund has enabled several *banjar*s to hire teachers to train their youths, children and women, and to buy new gamelan set and costumes and props, as a result, their performances are supposed to have acquired greater magnitude these days.

In the past too musicians, dancers, managers, costume makers, and members of the *sekaa* or the club would be paid for performances that they would make at ceremonies in one or other village. Some part of the money then too would go into a communal kitty, and the rest would be divided up among the group members. There would be a fierce pride as well as friendly competition among rival groups from different *sekaa*. A performer in the past too could perform independently of the *sekaa* (Dibia and Ballinger 2004: 15). McPhee writes that the money that clubs would make by performing "Legong" dances in the 1920s and 1930s would go "into treasury to be saved until the time of *galungan*, the week of feasts and holidays" and there would be "only a very small sum to share, for in the past six months the fund would have melted away on new costumes for the dancers, new gold leaf for the instruments, or a new set of head cloths for the members of the club" (2002: 42). And this tradition of managing art clubs and troupes has seen vibrant days in the context of the culture of performing for tourists of the present times. Since every village community is responsible for conducting ceremonies and rituals throughout the year, each member of the community needs to contribute some amount of money for oraganizing such occasions on a regular basis. Performing for tourists has eased their burden as it has enabled them to collect money for renovating and maintaining temples, and buying necessary items of offerings such as food, fruits and meat for rituals (see *fig.* 19).

I. Nyoman Martajaya, the *deśa* leader of the Padang Tegal village since 2003 heads "Sandi Suara Kecak," a *banjar*-based group and "Sandi Suara Barong and Kris Dance group," a village-based group. Both groups started to perform for tourists since 1994. Since representative of almost every family or household from the village comes to perform *Kecak* for tourists, as a leader of the *banjar* as well as performing groups Nyoman finds the evening of the performance a very apt occasion to communicate several issues related to village and *banjar* activities among villagers.[4] Similarly, "Desa Adat Sambahan Kecak" is also a *banjar*-based group from Sambahan village. It is led by Ketut Suartana, the leader of the village. Suartana told the researcher that the idea behind forming this particular *Kecak* group was to let the villagers feel a responsibility of doing something together. "Most of the villagers after their daily works in the field and office come home, watch television and sleep as part of their daily habit, but on the day of the performance, at least once a week, they put on the traditional Balinese attire, gather at their village temple, pray and become more spiritual and perform for

4. A personal interview with I. Nyoman Martajaya.

tourists."[5] As the members of the group, for that matter, the village community, the performers become more familiar with common agenda and works. They get time to discuss about carrying out ceremonies and festivals that keep on falling throughout the season. The evening that Suartana's group performs for tourists is also an occasion when a meeting between and among some 225 members of all generations coming from 150 families takes place. As the leader, Suartanta thinks performing for tourists has enabled him to be familiar with youths, most of them school and college goers so that he gets time to encourage them to learn and practise dance and music not only for tourists but also for making their culture stronger. He thinks that performing for tourists with local youths is a matter of joy and pride as it brings strong musical voice to the *Kecak* performance, and helps to make the local and traditional culture remain intact.

"Kecak and Fire Dance" presented by Taman community is led by Ketut Badra. Badra is also the leader of "Deśa Adat." This group, according to Badra, was formed to be different from others in Ubud not only in terms of performance but also in terms of its purpose. Money that this group makes by performing for tourists is mainly used for maintaining village temples and carrying out rituals of many kinds in the village. By not taking the money, the group members save it since they have to donate some money to run temple and community works almost every season as a matter of cultural rule and responsibility. Similarly, "Karma Desa Adat Junjugan Kecak" is another *banjar*-based group and is led by the *Deśa* leader, I Made Rajin. There are several more *banjar*-based groups in Ubud, and they run accordingly. As a matter of ethics it is regarded that a *banjar*-based group should not perform in the venue located in other *banjars*. This makes some *banjar*-based

5. A personal interview with Ketut Suartana.

groups always luckier since the number of tourists varies according to the location of the venue too. This further makes groups to develop and practise several policies to bring in tourists to their venues. *Banjar*-based groups located outside the central Ubud such as Junjugan and Buntuyan provide a free transportation service to tourists/audiences and provide a comparatively larger sum of commission to the ticket sellers.

As mentioned earlier, the number of the non-*banjar* based performing groups has increased in Ubud in the recent times. "Sanggar Pondok Pekak," a non-profit foundation located in Ubud leads three non-*banjar* based groups. Performers of "Pondok Pekak" groups come from several villages as far as Sukawati and Batuwan. "Pondok Pekak" also runs an international group of women's gamelan. Foreign ladies married to Balinese male and those living in Bali especially nearby Ubud for years meet regularly and rehearse and perform on several cultural events and occasions. I. Made Sumandera, the leader of the organization told the researcher that there are great many musicians and dancers available in Ubud for the kinds of dance and drama that "Pondok Pekak" groups stage for tourists but it is the very idea of bringing artists from different parts of Bali not only from Ubud that has remained a working principle of the foundation.[6]

"Theatre Raja Peni" is another non-*banjar*-based group. Artists are free to leave and join this group. More than fifty performers of this group do also perform for other groups in Ubud. Since its members come from many villages, it is "a more relaxed kind of group."[7] The leader, Ida Bagus Suteja told the researcher that performers who do not have time enough to play for this group simply can resign. Several

---

6. A personal interview with I. Made Sumandera.
7. An interview with Ida Bagus Suteja.

performers of the past have been replaced by perhaps better performers, he believes. "Padang Subadra Kecak" is another non-*banjar*-based group, and its members too keep on leaving and coming but greater the number and regularity of the members better remains the performance. To enhance spectacular and musical magnitude in it, a *Kecak* performance demands its members (at least 150 of them) remain familiar to the skill and the quality of each other's movement and voice.

The other thing about non-*banjar*-based performing groups in Ubud is that they are mostly membered and led by youths, especially the graduates from the university. "Balancing traditional village and family culture with the academic, many of our members are family members, neighbours, scholars as well as graduates of the Balinese University of the Arts. We like to refer to our respect for the traditional with an open heart for new ideas from global communities trans-culture,"[8] Kadek Dewi Aryani reads these lines from her diary as her group sets to stage the show for tourists in the *banjar* building located at the Monkey Forest football ground. Ms Aryani is a graduate from the ISI, and is also regarded as a famous "Taruna Jaya" dancer in Bali, and leads the recently formed group called "Nirtta Dewi" (see *fig.* 20). Groups membered by the youths, especially the graduates from the ISI often stage new or contemporary pieces to tourists. Since members of such groups are trained professionals in general, they are more mobile as they keep on performing and working with artists from abroad too. Putra, born in Ubud and trained by local maestros including Mandera from Peliatan and Jimat from Batuwan, and a graduate from the ISI, formed a group called "Semara Ratih," a non-*banjar*-based group in 1988 and started to perform for tourists from the same year. There are fifteen graduates from the ISI in this group. This group has taken

8. From Kadek Dewi Aryani's personal diary.

part in the *Bali Art Festival*s and competitions, and has won many awards, and is still regarded as the "number one"[9] group of Bali. It has worked and collaborated with many groups and musicians from abroad especially form Japan, America and Europe.

The presence of the ISI graduates in almost every group in Ubud makes one to realize the influence that the academy in Bali has carved out in the very sphere of the performance culture in Bali, for that matter, in Ubud too. Since the ISI graduates are mobile, they keep on performing for more than a group, and are popular among the Balinese as well as the tourists. Ni Wayan Pirlini, a comparatively busier dancer but not a graduate opines that had she been to the ISI, she could have been able to create new forms, and could have developed wider connections with the professionals and famous dance teachers and dancers from Bali, and could also have worked or collaborated with some famous dancers from abroad. She believes that Ubud is too small but there are many good performers and musicians and groups here. "Almost all artists from Bali love to perform in Ubud, but Ubud is a small space for everyone to show his or her talents"[10] says Ms Pirlini.

Banjar as a unit of organizational structure of Balinese village has played a very important role in giving the performance culture in Ubud a shape of an important order. *Banjar*-based groups make adjustment with each other regarding the day, venue and forms of dance and drama staged for the tourists. Many *banjar*s such as Junjugan and Peliatan do not want their local groups to perform more than once a week for the sake of maintaining quality in their performances. There are six groups in the Peliatan village, and each of them

9. From the Brochure of the group.

10. A personal interview with Ni Wayan Pirlini.

makes performance once a week. Their leaders tell that they do not want to copy Ubud by performing for tourists more than once a week and more than in a venue. Similarly, *Kecak* group from Junjugan village does not want to perform more than once a week for the same reason and the belief that the Peliatan-based groups hold.

The performance culture in Ubud has now become a zone of contestation between and among communities or *banjar*-based performing groups. Besides their worry and plan of drawing larger flow of tourists to their venues, *banjar* as well as non-*banjar*-based groups practise some ethics, poetics and politics in order to maintain identity and quality in their performances. Leaders of performing groups from Padang Tegal criticize the performing groups in Ubud for "hanging around" the Palace. They point out that eight groups from Ubud perform in the *Puri,* for that matter in the courtyard of the Palaces. Padang Tegal-based artists believe that they are more serious in managing the qualities in the performances made for tourists than those who perform in the Ubud palace. Similarly, the Peliatan-based groups point out that performing groups in Ubud unnecessarily borrow things from the academy. They criticize that Ubud has become almost like a "showroom" for the dance, drama and musical forms produced by the academia. Locals from the Junjugan village too do not like to perform *Kecak* more than once a week, because to do so would be like performing for the money. And, they do not want to make business out of the performance, thus give an impression that they are jealous of Ubud.[11] But Ubud has a comparatively greater number of venues for the performances. Professionals from different communities realise that they lack such centrally located spaces like that of Ubud.

---

11. An interview with I. Made Rajin.

Banjar as well as non-*banjar*-based performing groups use advertisement in a subtle manner to draw a greater flow of audience to their venue. Many groups such as "Tirta Sari," "Panca Arta," "Bina Remaja," "Sada Budaya," "Semara Ratih" and "Spirit of Bali" among others have performed abroad. They use "performed abroad" as a trope of their identity and use it to convince their audience about the quality of the performance that they have come to watch. Similarly, groups such as "Semara Ratih," "Mekar Sari" and "Ghenta Bhuwana Sari" among others have competed and won awards in the *Bali Art Festival*. They highlight their participation in such art festival as an achievement and use it as a means to promote their business. Many groups also use their individual member's professional identity to influence the audience and thereby make an attempt to create a greater flow of tourists to their venues. "Semara Ratih" mentions about its member or the leader Anak Agung Gde Putra, the *Baris Tunggal* dancer. Its brochure goes A.A. Putra was trained by I. Made Jimat before he graduated from the National Academy of Music and Dance in Denpasar, Bali, and is regarded as the most accomplished and famous young "Baris Dancer" (brochure). Similarly, the group "Topeng Jimat" performs a creation conceived by maestro Jimat in the courtyard of the Arma Museum. Jimat does not come to perform regularly for the tourists but his name is used as a means to draw the number of audience. "Pondok Pekak" children group presents "Geng Gong: Barong and Frog Dance," and its brochure claims that the particular dance-drama would have almost disappeared had they not popularized it. Groups which perform in the *Pura* Dalem Temple, the *Puri* Ubud, and the *Puri* and Balerung of Peliatan highlight the historicity and cultural importance associated with the venue as a policy to influence their audience. "Jegog Group (Suara Sakti)" from Buntuyun village asks its audience to come on the stage and dance to feel the music of the *Bamboo gamelan* in the last unit of its performance.

Ubud as Zones of Learning

Ubud is not only a marketsphere where performances for tourists are staged on a daily basis but also an important zone where dissemination of traditional, modern and contemporary Balinese dance, drama and musical forms takes place among the Balinese children, youths and women in a pragmatic manner. Members of all ages and sexes are seen practising and rehearsing Balinese dance and music on a regular basis in Ubud especially in a local *sanggar*, a name given to dance and music studio that provides certificate of a certain academic value. Though *sanggar* was first to appear in Denpasar, it has become more popular in Ubud these days. There are five *sanggars* in Ubud. "Sanggar Chudamani" located in the Pongosekan village has five active composers of "advanced ranks of creativity," and it teaches traditional and contemporary music, dance, and shadow/puppet theatre to children, youths and women. "Sanggar Chudamani" is also one of the few organizations in Bali that teaches gamelan to girls — a realm that until recently was reserved for males. This *sanggar* has made debut on several things but one of its "signature pieces is *Wayang Listrik* (Electric Wayang), a new form of shadow puppetry" (Dibia and Ballinger 2004: 39). It is also regarded as the biggest zone of dissemination of Balinese dance and music as it provides training to several groups of children, youths, women and men. The learners or practitioners in this *sanggar* do not have to pay any fee but the teachers are paid as the Ford Foundation has sponsored "Sanggar Chudamani's" many programmes for several years. Mostly, the classes start from three in the afternoon to eight at night. Nyoman Carita, the famous dance creator and teacher from the ISI takes classes here. I. Dewa Putu Rai one of the managers of the *sanggar* told the researcher that the *sanggar* does not follow the ISI pedagogics but mixes several styles and tries to create something new in its form and spirit.[12]

Every Sunday morning and on Tuesday and Wednesday afternoons, I.G.A. Raka Rasmi (see *fig.* 21), the first "Bumble Bee" dancer, someone trained by Mario in 1951, along with her three assistants is seen busy teaching over one hundred children in the "Arma Kumara Sanggar" in the Peliatan village. The yard, lobby and hall behind the reception counter of the Arma Museum are virtually occupied by children who mostly come from Peliatan, Mas and Ubud villages (see *fig.* 22). This *sanggar* is another biggest zone of dissemination of music that the researcher could see in his nine-month long research. The name of I.G.A. Raka Rasmi, the Peliatan dance style associated with her, and the Bali-famous venue has made the place a very vibrant zone of teaching, for that matter, disseminating the Balinese dance, drama and musical forms. Groups that perform for tourists in the venue of the Arma Museum contribute 10 per cent of their income to the *sanggar*. And the money is used to pay the teachers and to maintain the venue.

Similarly, the "Sanggar Tedung Agung" is another very active *sanggar* and is located in the *Puri* Ubud. It is supported by the economic contribution made by the four groups which perform for tourists in the courtyard of the *Puri* Ubud. This *sanggar* was established in 1993 and is being presided over by the youngest prince of the *Puri*. It provides free lessons to the children from local communities three days a week. The "Pondok Pekak" is another *sanggar* that has got two groups which perform for tourists, and one "International Women Gamelan group" that performs at different ceremonies. The *sanggar* carries its regular activities of training children from

12. A personal interview with I. Dewa Putu Rai.

the fund supported by its own performing groups. It has got a dream and vision of letting children from Ubud have an opportunity of practising almost every kind of music and dance forms available in Bali. The "Luh Luwih" is another important *sanggar* in the Pangosekan village. It was set to look after women's activities, and is led by Mrs Suarti, the famous woman entrepreneur of Bali. It has got two performing groups: one formed out of the senior performers who have already performed in many countries. This group performs on different art and cultural festivals and competitions held in Bali and other islands of Indonesia. The second group has just been formed and has started to perform for tourists in Ubud since November 2006. The *sanggar* is managed through a small sum of economic contribution that its groups make by performing for tourists in Ubud, Bali and abroad.

Similarly, the "Balerung Mandera Srinertya Waditra" established by A.A. Gede Oka Dalem (one of Agung Mandera's sons) though is not *sanggar*, provides free lessons to children from the Peliatan village and around. This centre has an aim of preserving classical music and dance forms originated in the Peliatan. The *Balerung* has got three groups that perform for tourists. Each group contributes 10 per cent of its total income to maintain the venue, instruments, and importantly to teach children the dance and music on every Sunday morning. Children here like elsewhere are not charged any money. Dalem told the researcher that he does not want the Peliatan style of dance and music to be replaced by the ISI or the Denpasar style not because he does not like the latter but because he wants the Balinese performing arts and cultures to maintain its multiple colours within.[13] Moreover, the Peliatan-based dance and musical forms are the ones that his father

13. A personal interview with A.A. Gede Oka Dalem.

and his father's friends created some eighty years ago, and were the ones that the world saw for the first time and understood the quality of the Balinese performing art as such, therefore, he thinks that there is a greater exigency of keeping them vibrant.

Thus performing for tourists has enabled the locals in Ubud and the villages around create a fund and manage it in disseminating traditional as well as modern and contemporary Balinese dance and musical forms among the local children, youths and women. This can be taken as an important move to keep local art and culture intact.

Women Performers in Ubud

Compared to its past, Ubud has become more artist-friendly especially to its women performers now. Most of the girl performers after they get married do find it hard to perform on a regular basis. But the reason and opportunity of performing for tourists has made the married women, the former artists, more active as they are engaged in forming and managing their own *gamelan* groups. Most of the women artists who perform for tourists in Ubud are in their forties and fifties. They are accompanied by the dancers of the age of their children and grandchildren on the stage. They have performed on cultural occasions for decades, but performing for tourists has made them to go through a rigorous process of rehearsal. Four women *gamelan* groups including the one that was going through rigorous rehearsal during my research period perform for tourists on a regular basis in Ubud. "Mekar Sari," a group that performs in Peliatan at Balerung stage has got thirty-five musicians and twenty-five dancers as its members. When this group started to perform for tourists in 1989, it became the news in Bali, and many people used to come to watch this group's performance.

Swastika Raka, an instructor of *gamelan* music of several women groups believes that there is demand as well as pride in forming a women *gamelan* group these days in Ubud. He as the instructor of the new women's *gamelan* group that was going through rehearsal told the researcher that the particular group will not be allowed to perform for tourists until a "standard" is maintained in every piece of dance, drama and musical forms that the group is supposed to stage for tourists. The group, as the researcher was told, was rehearsing some traditional musical pieces that are very hard to practise. Raka opines that in the past in Ubud, women were not considered as good musicians. Women artists in the past danced till they were married. Many of them would stop dancing for ever. But women hold good abilities and discipline required for practising and performing traditional as well as modern Balinese musical forms. "Girls when they start dancing and practising music do it marvellously well. But when they become women they feel nervous in performing and practising music. Now everywhere in Bali, there is a demand for women's *gamelan* group"[14] says Raka.

Similarly, the "Pondok Pekak Sanggar" runs an international women *gamelan* group. Its women musicians and dancers come from different nations, and many of them are married to Balinese men or have been living in Bali for several years. This group performs for temple ceremonies only. It has performed at several festivals and art competitions held in Bali, and has its own schedule of rehearsal and performances. The "Luh Luwih Women's Gamelan" group was formed to increase the frequency of meeting between and among women performers. Temple ceremonies do bring women performers together only for a few days in a year. But once they start performing for tourists, the meetings between and among

14. A personal interview with Swastika Raka.

women artists become much more frequent. Since they perform for tourists mostly once a week, they need to meet and rehearse on a regular basis. Desak Nyoman Suarti, the winner of 2006 Kartini Award, a national and prestigious award of Indonesia, is the leader of this group. She thinks that only after the members of all ages and sexes start to practise dance and music, the performance culture can remain more vibrant. Moreover, women are eager to perform and they do it very well.[15] At least one or the other women's *gamelan* group performs for tourists in Ubud everyday. Moreover, every performing group including the *Kecak* group has some female dancers in it. This makes one to realize a fact that the number of women performers in Ubud has increased in recent years.

University Graduates and Local Performers

Artists from the Peliatan village might go and perform in Ubud. But many things depend on their talents. It is a very difficult and challenging task for the dancers and musicians trained in the Peliatan style to go and perform in Ubud where the Denpasar or the ISI style dance and musical forms mostly rule. Many senior artists from the Peliatan also argue that the Peliatan style dance and drama were already famous before the ISI started to invent and teach its own styles to its students. They blame that the ISI has modified some of the old and popular dance and musical forms with the purpose of addressing commercial need. They realize that the Peliatan style is a bit more difficult to acquire, and it demands more energy than the ISI style dance usually demands. "Dances in the Peliatan style are more classical, and they demand rigorous practice and disciplines,"[16] argues I Wayan Swatuma. The following remarks made by Racki, a Western scholar on the

15. A personal interview with Desak Nyoman Suarti.

16. A personal interview with I. Wayan Swatuma.

Balinese music dance and music, can also be linked with the discourse put by the artists from the Peliatan village. Teaching pupils according to the traditional pedagogy, Racki puts, "does not stem from an intellectual analysis of movement and music, but rather on the student's kinesthetic sensations." And this pedagogic tradition "directly addresses the intuitive being of the young artist to become a living temple of the spirit" (Racki 1998: 19-20). Performers from the Peliatan village highlight this very mode of teaching and practising dance.

Since "Gunung Sari" has performed for decades, it holds a rich heritage of dance and musical forms in the Peliatan style. Mario, the great genius of Bali who brought revolutionary changes in the Balinese dances too had worked for this group. Most of the dances in the *Kebyar* style that this group performs for tourists these days were revolutionary creations of their kind in the history of the Balinese performance culture. Thus a style called the Peliatan dance and drama has come into existence for many decades in Bali. Groups and performers in the Peliatan village feel this heritage and are dedicated to keep it alive. "We in Peliatan do not have any fixed notation, rules and exercise books and theories like the ones that the ISI has developed for its students," says Dalem, the leader of "Tirta Sari" group. He further argues that in the Peliatan, teachers and students believe in the essence of communication between musicians and dancers: "ISI has its counting system, a rigorous modern mode of teaching but here (in Peliatan) we do it in natural style. We have our sense of movements and expressions. We practise the same dance and music forms which the ISI teaches to its students but we do them in a different style. We believe in the real *Kebyar* style that a dancer cannot remain free in movements and expressions without communicating with musicians."[17] Dalem and his fellow

17. An personal interview with A.A. Gde Oka Dalem.

teachers and leaders of performing groups in the Peliatan village believe and argue that the ISI or the Denpasar dance and drama forms do not have any problems of survival because a number of students throughout Bali, Indonesia and the world come every year to learn in the ISI, and disseminate them accordingly whereas if the dancers and musicians from the Peliatan do not keep on practising dance and drama in their styles, the Peliatan styles can disappear for ever. Hendrawan, the leader of "Gunung Sari" states, "We follow the non-academic style. We cannot maintain our past and heritage of Peliatan if we start practising others' styles. But if others want to learn dance and drama in the Peliatan style we welcome them. We also do not mind if our members decide to learn dance and music in the ISI style but when we perform in Peliatan, we have to do and always try to do things in the Peliatan styles. Our dance and music styles are in practice since 1920s, we cannot forget them now at any cost."[18]

Dalem demonstrated differences between the Peliatan and the ISI dance styles by showing a few dance movements to the researcher to show that the Peliatan "Legong" dancers do not bend their bodies in angular form as the ones trained in the ISI or the Denpasar styles usually do. "Peliatan Legong" dancers are more expressive, and their bodies keep on moving up and down, it is not as codified as the Denpasar or the ISI style demands, says Kadek Dewi Aryani, the ISI graduate and the leader of "Nritta Dewi Gamelan" group who used to perform for the Peliatan-based groups in the past too. "The Peliatan-styled dance demands its practitioners take in personal expression whereas the dances in the ISI and the Denpasar style demand its performers express everything out. The Denpasar or the ISI style is softer whereas the Peliatan style is more dynamic"[19] says Ms Aryani. Mrs Rakka, now 67 years old, was

18. A personal interview with Hendrawan.

19. A personal interview with Kadek Dewi Aryani.

the first "Bumble Bee" dancer in Bali. Mario taught her this dance in 1952 for a month. She was ten years old then. The time the "Bumble Bee" dance was created was the time when the classical dances such as "Legong" and "Arja" dominated the performance culture of Bali. This new creation of Mario made everyone curious about it and was taken as a new piece of good work. It had lots of movements and expressions and became popular in no time. She teaches the same Peliatan style of dance as she was trained it. She argues that the ISI or the Denpasar-styled dances are also good but the Peliatan style is different and she wants to keep them alive.[20] Tjokorde Alit Dalem, the leader of "Semara Madya Kecak" group argues, "We do not take anything from the ISI and Denpasar. We have our own style. Academic people want to bring uniformity in dance and drama especially those presented for tourists. It is very ironic that those who lead the academia these days are the children of the parents who learnt and practised dance and music in Peliatan and got fame and recognition in Bali."[21]

Putra, the leader of "Spirit of Bali" and "Semara Ratih" groups is one of the busiest performers of Bali. Putra, himself a graduate from the ISI and also someone trained by local maestros like Jimat and late Mandera of Peliatan, believes that it is best to learn from local senior dancers and musicians in a social and cultural atmosphere. He thinks that learning dance and music through taking classes in any art colleges does not allow one to experience the rich cultural and traditional mode of learning and practising Balinese dance and drama forms. He complains about the teaching methodology that the academy in Bali follows:

---

20. A personal interview with I.G.A. Raka Rasmi.

21. A personal interview with Tjokorde Alit Dalem.

> Academy in Bali uses monotonous mode of counting movements: one, two, three, four, five and six, a very mathematical way of measuring movements of Balinese dance. As a result dances have become more formulaic. When I started to learn dance from senior artists from different villages, I was not made or asked to count movement, it did never occur to me as an important process of learning Balinese dance and musical forms. I tried to learn every gesture and beat of music with a sense of feeling. It was the very art of articulating inner feeling through gestures and movements than creating anything that is visible was what I was taught by my local gurus.[22]

I. Wayan Jaya Marta, himself a graduate from the ISI and someone trained in the Peliatan village, now works as a co-ordinator of three performing groups in the Arma museum. He argues that there are fundamental differences between the Peliatan and the ISI style of dance and drama as the former executes gentle movement whereas the latter executes athletics and sports-like movement. He opines that one can still call the Peliatan dance spiritual because the performers are taught to feel or evoke some spiritual power on the stage which is important because artists must feel that they are performing for gods first and then only to human audience either tourists or locals. He blames that many "Pendet," known as "welcome dances," in Ubud and other areas look as if they are created only with the purpose of doing it for tourists as the performers in such dances do not feel the presence of god on stage. "We as Peliatan-based performers vow to evoke spiritual aura on the stage whether we perform for tourists or locals or gods. We do not hesitate to call the dances in the Peliatan style as more complete as they need more energy, are longer and need more concentration"[23] says Marta.

---

22. A personal interview with A.A. Putra.
23. A personal interview with I. Wayan Jaya Marta.

However, performers in Ubud, as far as my research revealed to me, do not work with this sense of dialectics that the performers in the Peliatan usually do. They agree that dances in the Peliatan style do exist but the dances in the ISI styles are easier to practise. Teachers who are available to teach dance and drama, those who come to check the quality in the performances made for the tourists and those who approve and give license to new groups to perform for tourists in Ubud are associated with the ISI or academy in Bali in one way or the other. Most of the groups in Ubud perform one or the other creation of the teachers from the ISI as a part of maintaining canonicity. Therefore, performers in Ubud work in a negotiation with academic and bureaucratic authority.

But, on the other hand, some professionals opine that those who perform for the tourists in Ubud need follow neither academic nor local style but must carve out new styles. Performers performing the role of a clown in *Kecak* or other dance and drama forms need to execute local as well as global jokes to address the interest of tourists who do not want to get lost in the jungle of words which even the Balinese themselves do not understand since many dances and dramas are based on the epics *Mahābhārata* and *Rāmāyaṇa* as well as other older myths that use the Kawi, the ancient Javanese Sanskrit. I. Made Gender, the local Dalang from the Monkey Forest Area believes that "what tourists want is action-packed puppet show: a bit and piece of humour in English here and there." Tourists as audience love to laugh and get entertained. One can argue that such psyche of audience makes the *Dalang*, the puppet master to invent something that is highly entertaining while doing with something very Balinese traditional form of art. Gender told the researcher that the tourists as audience have "every right to get entertained," and there is no harm in making them laugh. Therefore, there is a need of a creative *Dalang* who can create something that is new while presenting something that is very old. "The ISI graduates and even senior artists who perform at rituals too need to learn an art of improvizing and creating some flavour and scenes to entertain tourists,"[24] says Gender.

Future of Ubud's Performance Culture

Tourists alone do not shape the future for the performance culture in Ubud. Group leaders and artists interviewed argue that much depends on the music instructor as he or she knows how to pass on art and skills of practising music and dance into the mind and the body of performers across generation. Critics and researchers on the Balinese performance culture have pointed out the importance of this very cultural mode of disseminating traditional Balinese dance and drama forms. The group leaders and instructors interviewed argue that performers/professionals are the custodians of the very "artworld" of the performance culture that they have created in Ubud and therefore they too need to watch each other's performances made for tourists to develop a culture of criticism from within. Swastika Raka believes that performers should not work with a feeling of competition between and among groups but, importantly, must practise a responsibility of creating the performance culture of a greater magnitude in Ubud. He argues that performers need to realize that they should not remain happy in showing what is popular and striking for tourists but must learn to expand the very world of the Balinese performance culture as well as act out a fact that the quality in the performances does not emanate from the amount of money invested in forming a group and money spent in buying musical instruments and costumes. Moreover, groups should not make attempts to survive from the talent

24. A personal interview with I. Made Gender.

of a few performers but should practise a reality that greater the number of professional performers better remains the domain of performance culture,[25] says Raka.

Group leaders and performers in Ubud believe that it is not only the talents of a few individual professionals but more importantly the very culture of living, working, and helping each other that has helped the performance culture in Ubud reach to "this" state. The force that combines members within a group and beyond is lacking, many senior artists in Ubud complain about. Professionals should also work with raw or learners. If professionals occupy all the space, they will remain enemy to the very culture that they want to create. Therefore, fresh and professionals should work together and experience the greater bond, otherwise the performance culture in Ubud will lack the very ethos of the Balinese performing culture, many leaders argue.

Senior local artists from Peliatan and Ubud argue that the *taksu* is another force that will determine the future of the performance culture practised for tourists in Ubud. "Number of tourists may go up and down but if artists do not try to achieve the state of *taksu*, it will bring decadence in the performance culture in Ubud,"[26] argues Ms Aryani. *Taksu* is an aesthetically as well as spiritually loaded term. Racki writes that one can receive *taksu* only after he or she achieves a state of living temple of spirit which is possible through a teaching of guru by correcting and adjusting the pupil's limbs, arms and legs as part of showing him or her dance over and over again (Racki 1998: 19-20). Racki further writes, it is "mastery of dance technique," "a harmonious bond between the music and the dance" that can help the artist attain the state of *taksu*.

---

25. A personal interview with Swastika Raka.

26. A personal interview with Kadek Dewi Aryani .

And for it, the artists should make "offerings and pray under the guidance of a *pedanda*" (1998: 20-21).

Thus the culture of performing for tourists has given an important dynamism to the very culture of disseminating traditional and modern Balinese dance, drama and musical forms among local children, youths and women in Ubud. It has also set new roles for the very custodians of the performance culture in Bali as they have set to act out their being member of the *banjar* in a new cultural context. They have used the very act of performing for tourists as a medium to intensify their ceremonies, rituals, dance and drama — thus the very performance culture. It has also defined the performers as "critical" intellectuals as they defy academic influences in the performance culture of Bali through highlighting the values and the significance of local styles. This culture has also brought university graduates as well as local performers into a forum where they can learn from each other and realize the importance of maintaining diversities from within. Moreover, performing for tourists has made the custodians of the performance culture in Ubud realize the problematics ahead, and this realization has resulted in a serious engagement from within the very culture of performing for tourists.

Finally, the culture of performing for tourists has made local artists to realise the importance of practising this very culture as it can give the art and skills of practising dance, drama and musical performances a greater flow across the generations and the sexes. The money that the tourists pay as audience for the show has directly helped the Ubudians to create some important zones of dissemination of traditional, modern and contemporary Balinese dance and musical forms, and thereby helped the very culture of performing not only for tourists but also for locals and their gods to secure a greater future. This has made one to realise the need of redefining not only tourists as audience of the traditional performance culture but also the performances made for them as well as the artists who perform for them, which is the subject of the next chapter.

6

Redefining Audience, Performances and Performers

Tourists and the Performance Culture

THUS tourists as audience become an important agency in the continuity and change process of the Balinese performance culture in Ubud. Crossing through several channels of networks created by agents of tourism business, from travel agency to local guide, hotel crew to hawker, not only tourists/audience but even creators, practitioners and disseminators of traditional, modern and contemporary Balinese dance, drama and musical forms themselves finally arrive at different venues in Ubud every evening. A tourist, though often theorized as a "meta-tourist" or a "post-tourist" (Urry 2002: 91), someone who is conscious of being a tourist in a certain point of time and space in his or her life, or one who is always in the process of being a tourist, makes several important things happen in the domain of the "artworld" of a cultural nature in Ubud. Similarly, when performers in a specific cultural site set to perform for tourists, as the performance culture in Ubud reveals to us, they become not only "meta-performers," someone who are conscious of doing it for some kinds of audience but also "critical" performers who hold power to define and redefine their profession, art and culture. And, performances made for tourists, though often canonized as "meta-local" and "meta-touristic," can become an aesthetic and intellectual exercise that can problematize the hitherto established canons about traditional Balinese dance, drama, music, tourists and local performers. Performance culture practised for tourists, as far as my research in Ubud has revealed to me, has heralded new roles to the researchers, academicians, practitioners and custodians of performance art and culture in Bali. Traditional dance, drama and musical forms are going through a process of re-definition, thus enabling one to experience the very heritage of the performance culture in Bali as an "ever present arena" and not a thing of the past only. Importantly, this culture of performing for tourists in Ubud has created several zones of: dissemination, learning and teaching of dance, drama and musical forms across generations and sexes within the village communities.

Before I set to analyse the paradoxes inherent in the praxis of differentiating tourist from other types of audience of the performance culture of traditional order in this chapter, I would like to raise some questions: Who are the ideal audience of the traditional dance, drama and musical forms? Can locals, since they are locals, therefore be regarded as the most authentic audience of such art forms? Do anthropologists or researchers, since they are scholars, be taken as valid audience of such art forms? Do expatriates become "authentic" audience of such performances as they manage to influence locals and their cultures? Were the tourists of the past days luckier as they watched dance and drama in the older forms? Should the tourists of the present times be regarded as naïve audience of the cultural performances staged for them simply because they belong to contemporary times? Does a performance become "unauthentic" simply because tourists of the present times have come to watch it? Do performers feel guilty when they perform their cultural dance and drama forms for the tourists? Who holds the power to judge about the quality of performances made for tourists — tourists themselves or practitioners or researchers or academicians? Should the very qualifier 'meta' that is often attached with tourists, performers and performances in the context of the cultural tourism be taken as a tag of decadence or a process of intellectual and creative transformation that every individual and art form manages to achieve in the post-modern context? Are not performances staged either for tourists or locals the artefacts that "need to be made, in some manner of deliberate, even self-conscious creation, then, in order to be artifacts at all, rather than accidents or natural objects" (Wartofsky 1980: 2)?

Problematics of Canon

I would like to address the questions raised above with reference to the culture of performing for tourists in Ubud as discussed in earlier chapters. The history of the Balinese performance culture reveals to us that the academia and the national cultural policy makers found it as a matter of exigency to create canons about the Balinese dance and drama since it was found some ritualistic or religious dances were staged for the tourists. Several rounds of seminar on the issue of sacred and secular nature of the Balinese dance and drama forms took place in the 1970s. Finally, it was decided that not all but only a few "selective" dances and dramas are subject of performances for tourists. And dances that are watched by tourists must be interpreted as secular ones. But when the dance and drama that are performed for tourists are performed on cultural occasions as part of the temple ceremonies, they are to be called *bebali* or ceremonial. This academic and bureaucratic intervention, no matter how important was it from an insider's perspective, was a deliberate attempt of defining the Balinese dance, drama and musical forms into three categories: sacred, ceremonial and secular. And tourists of the present times in Bali become eternally secular audience though the dance and drama they watch can remain both sacred and ceremonial, and secular. Academic and bureaucratic offices check the formalistic structures and the "standardness" of the performances made for the tourists these days in Bali. Groups performing for tourists stage also the dance drama created in academia including those which are thematically socialistic and nationalistic, thus loved by the bureaucrats as well. Thus this "artworld" of performing for tourists in Ubud has become a domain of hegemony, domination, control, manipulation, "which are real features of the politics of art, no less than are aesthetic determinations of value and propriety, progress and innovation, banality and pseudo-art" (Wartofsky 1980: 7).

This politics of canonizing Balinese dance and drama forms into such categories has put the tourists of the present times at the bottom level of the hierarchy of audiences. It has also promulgated a judgemental view that the performances made for the tourists always remain less "authentic." This canon assumes that the very process that a tourist of the present times goes through before he or she becomes the audience of the cultural performance in the local site is an unauthentic one, and gives continuity to the same hypothesis that, given the condition of being a tourist, an audience, as ephemeral as the very performance staged, "there is neither a felt necessity nor an opportunity to create mutual trust" (Cohen 1984: 379). This lack of "mutual trust" between the performers and the audiences is taken as the qualifier of the artefacts created and practised for the tourists. But this hypothesis does not bother to address the issue of "critical" power which performers as custodians of performance culture can possess and live with.

Anthropologists and Tourists

As tourists arrive at a venue to watch performances made for them, they enter the Balinese aesthetic zone that belonged to the anthropologists or researchers in the past. The performances made in ritual contexts, dance and drama of the rare and the almost disappearing kinds in Bali have always remained as research topics for the anthropologists and researchers. Anthropologists are credited for making some important daring adventures to the world yet unknown to tourists. Often praised for speaking for the sake of the "natives," anthropologists assert their authority "to represent the lives of their subjects" and take "great pains to distinguish themselves, on the one hand, from tourists, and, on the other, from stationary missionaries and colonial officials" (Rosaldo 1986: 96). The Western researchers and anthropologists to Bali have played similar important roles as their discourses on the Balinese art and culture became counter arguments to the ones made and circulated by the agents of the Dutch Empire and missionaries in the past. As discussed in the third chapter of the book, researchers over a hundred years have worked on the Balinese performance culture, and have described, as researchers themselves say, how an individual visitor needs to "scan a variety of sights/sites" (Urry 2002: 150-51) in Bali. Many of the researchers in the past even worked with the local artists and helped the latter to create new art forms. In Turner's terms, they in Bali have tried to know the art and culture of Balinese through entering the latter's "performances and learning their grammars and vocabularies" (Turner qtd. in Schechner and Appel, 1997: 1), and their number has reached as many as one hundred a year (Vickers 1996: 189) in the present times.

Since tourists are not anthropologists, they are often told that they miss "real" or "authentic" performance, and the one they arrive to watch becomes always "touristic." Tourists too are given "grammars" and "vocabularies" of performances in a form of brochure in English, for that matter, tourists' language. Anthropologists in the past could and would watch the drama and dance that the tourists watch these days only after waiting for several months, by then only they were supposed to encounter the "ethnic" culture and would create images of the Balinese performance culture accordingly. But the tourists of the present times come just in time to watch the performances staged for them, and leave the venue after the shows are over. Anthropologists probably would record performances minutely, and take some extensive interviews with local performers; tourists take as many photos of the shows as they like, and too love to talk to the performers. Most of the performances made for tourists are staged in the temple yard in Ubud. As the show for the tourists is about to begin, the local priest appears on stage and performs a round of ritual of purifying the stage (see *fig.* 23), and again appears at the end of the show to pacify performers, especially the possessed fire dancer and other performers. To the surprise of everyone including the anthropologists of the past, the tourists of the present times live through a culture where and when it is affirmed that "ethnicity" too can be invented and staged. The assumption that a community and its individual members as "owners" of ritual and liturgy have "authority to introduce, under certain culturally determined conditions, elements of novelty from time to time into socially inherited deposit of ritual customs" (Turner 1982: 31) makes one to realize the fact that tourists of the present times encounter the custodians of the Balinese performance culture of different time and set of minds. Moreover, performing traditional, modern, and contemporary Balinese dance, drama and musical forms for the tourists in Ubud enables one to realize an important fact that "ethnicity" associated with such art forms too is a subject of change and continuity, not something that is "simply passed on from generation to generation, taught and learned; it is something dynamic, often unsuccessfully, repressed or avoided" (Fischer, 1986: 195).

As discussed in the earlier chapters, the history and the heritage of the Balinese performance culture shows that the aesthetic revolution called the *Kebyar* of the early twentieth century itself was a major driving force for stimulating the local Balinese artists to create the dramatic, ritually free, secular and shorter dance drama forms. In the course of time, such "free" dance, drama and musical forms have become culturally and spiritually important as they are performed at different temple ceremonies too. Several performances designed with the purpose of performing for tourists "use similar ritual procedures as the ceremonies that inspired them, be they the presentation of offerings or the use of consecrated accessories" (Picard 1966: 160). Importantly, the researchers who lived in Ubud for a couple of years in the period between the Wars, are often taken as the pioneers of the cultural tourism as they helped the local artists to invent new forms and explore professionalism in Ubud. And, the tourists now have become the patrons of great many traditional dance, drama and musical forms that the researchers on Balinese art and culture so much loved and talked about in the past. Thus tourists and anthropologists, for that matter, researchers on the Balinese performance culture, evoke each other. They are not the members of the opposite team.

Expatriates and Tourists

As mentioned in the second chapter, out of 47,000 expatriates living in Bali, 8,400 live in Ubud (Murdoch 2002: 7-8). During my nine-month long research-stay, I came across several expatriates who often criticize about the "touristic" performances made in Ubud and the villages around. They argue that such a culture of performing for tourists has brought in fragmentation, and reduced and "truncated" the local and traditional Balinese dance, drama and musical forms (Murdoch 2002: 7-8). Expatriates since they have lived for decades in Bali and are known and respected among locals, they are often invited as guests to watch ceremonies that take place in the temple. They take this opportunity as a trope of power, i.e. being "authentic" audience of some "authentic" Balinese dance and drama performances. Though they do not complain about the quality of the performances staged for the tourists on a daily basis in Ubud, they argue that such performances lack *taksu*, a trope of aesthetic and spiritual power. *Taksu* is taken as "an energy, a type of spiritual charisma that exceptional artists (and healers) are blessed with" and has "little to do with technical precision." Moreover, it is as ephemeral and epiphanic as performance itself and a performer can attain *taksu* at "one performance and the following night fall flat" (Dibia and Ballinger 2004: 11). Thus the *taksu* is not a fixed quality attached with certain performances and performers.

In this process of getting equipped with some tropes of power, i.e. knowledge on the Balinese performance culture, expatriates are joined by the tourism business-makers and regular-comer-tourists to Bali. And together they regard *taksu*, Ṛṣi Mārkaṇḍeya, Walter Spies, McPhee and other names of great stature from the "Balipedia" as affirmation of their knowledge or mastery over the "grammar" and "vocabulary" of the Balinese performance culture. They take such local, spiritual and aesthetic tropes if not to dominate but surely not to be dominated by tourists. Though expatriates do not discourage tourists from watching "touristic" performances, they are not found watching such shows. Many of them have narratives of their own about their encounter with some "authentic" Balinese dance and drama. They mostly narrate about their experience that they accumulated by watching performances at a certain night in a certain temple far from the usual place where tourists go to watch, and mind it, there were not many Balinese audience either, and the performance was the "best" they have ever watched in Bali. But to their shock and surprise, they do not come to watch the performances staged for the tourists on a regular basis to find the same performers and performances that they watched at temple ceremonies. On many occasions, the temple ceremony and dance and drama related to it take place in the same venue where tourists go to watch on a regular basis.

Tourists of the Past and the Present

Tourists of the past days are also often taken as the luckier audience since they had had an opportunity of watching the art and culture of Bali when it was not 'spoilt' at all. This hypothesis emanates partly from the very process that the tourists in the past would go through before they would reach to the venue and become the audience. The tourists who would come to Bali in the past had to walk hours to reach the venue whereas the tourists of the present times may find the "same" dance and drama in the same venue, not necessarily in the same style that the formers used to watch. But the tourists of the present times belong to a different time and culture of travelling and "continuity and change" state of the local Balinese cultures and arts. These days the roads in Bali are busy. Tourists do not have to walk across the paddy field to reach the venue. They do not encounter the "shrieks of the monkeys" and the "croaking of the frogs" on the way to the venue either. Decades back roads, field and atmosphere in Bali were different but to look for the same ambience or atmosphere is to look for something impossible, an Oedipal hunt.

The atmosphere of "velvety black night," "thirty miles long drive," "a narrow winding road," paddy-fields "flooded with water and into the recesses of jungle gorges," and "nocturnal slumbering" of monkeys (Clune and Stephensen 1994: 246) were the moments that the audience of those days had to pass through before they would finally arrive at the venue. But to tell the tourists or the audience of the present times that they miss such of those days is to miss the dynamics of the change and continuity that a culture as well as an individual lives through. Thus the discourse of "authentic" local performance functions as the politics to make the tourists of the present times to act out the persona of the tourists and the researchers of the past days. Ironically, the tourism business in Bali in such "natural" days was not run by and for the Balinese but by the colonial agents and power holders for their own race and government or company as "the sale of tourist objects, carved wooden heads of dancers and so on, was run discretely through a few small shops mainly owned by Europeans" (Vickers, 1989: 97). Researchers and locals of the present times state it with an emphasis that the temples, ceremonies and dance and drama in Bali these days have become larger and more spectacular. Performing arts in Bali have become more vibrant. Many old dance drama and musical forms have given place to their newer versions. And, there is a strong ground for an argument that Balinese performance culture has seen more prosperous days in the recent years. Thus the tourists of the present times are not "unlucky" audience of the Balinese performance culture as they are often claimed to be.

Local Audience and Tourists

Locals and tourists do not form the audience structures of binary opposition as they are often taken or thought to be. Critics and researchers on the Balinese performance art and culture argue that detaching dance and drama from their ritualistic context was developing a new sense of aesthetics of modern nature known as the *Kebyar* for the Balinese themselves. And this detachment, initiated by the Balinese for their own purposes, required the intercession of an external gaze, that of the tourists first, and then that of the Indonesians (Picard 1996: 134). When "Bumble Bee" was created by Mario for the Peliatan-based group "Gunung Sari" for its 1952 world famous America tour, this piece was thought to have brought an intervention into the gaze of the local audience who then were mostly used to watching the classical and traditional dance and drama in Peliatan. Mrs Raka, now 67 years old, the first "Bumble Bee" dancer, told the researcher that even the locals then took this new piece of good work with wonder as it had lots of movements and expressions, and, in no time, it became popular among locals too.[1]

Tourists started coming to Bali from the 1930s on a regular basis. Several sacred or *wali* as well as some secular forms were performed for them in some villages on an almost daily basis, without regard for the calendar of religious festivals (Bandem and deBoer 1995: 127-28). Moreover, new forms of dance and drama were invented to be performed for tourists in hotels. Some of such creations of the past have now "assumed a life and place of their own in the spectrum of Balinese performance, and have been, to some extent, authenticated through constant repetition" (Bandem and deBoer 1995: 128). Moreover, on the day of the temple ceremony one comes across tourists, locals, expatriates and researchers on Bali, almost all of them dressed up in Balinese traditional dress *sarong* gathered together in the temple precinct to watch ceremonial dance and drama. Locals as audience for such art forms keep on moving, chat with each other and some "lads" manage to fall in love, and the

1. Interview with I.G.A. Raka Rasmi.

ceremonial occasion itself becomes a part of the ongoing life of the locals. Similarly, tourists and other non-Balinese also meet, talk and manage to share not necessarily only the experience of watching the very Balinese dance and culture but many more. Thus one encounters a picture of "glocal" and "leaky" Ubud, for that matter Bali, at such temple ceremonies when and where hierarchy of audience for local cultural performances created and disseminated by the academia and the bureaucrats in Bali break into. Tourist, among other audience made up of locals, expatriates, business makers and researchers on Bali on such occasion no matter how little he or she manages to understand the Balinese performance becomes or gets the title of the patron as the discussion in the earlier chapter of the book reveals out. He or she becomes not just a "meta-tourist" but a patron of the great many art forms that locals, anthropologists and the tourists of bygone days have loved, watched and worked on.

Nature of Art and the Importance of Performing for Tourists

Performances made for the tourists in Ubud are artefacts, not merely "touristic" entities. Makers of these "artefacts" for the tourists are the "artworlders" of the performance culture of a vibrant nature. These "artworlders" include great many senior performers, some of them in their seventies — artists who have been practicing dance, drama and musical forms for over six decades — university graduates, world famous Balinese dancers and musicians, amateurs, learners, business makers, farmers and intellectuals. Researchers, historians and locals believe that many of the "artworlders" in Ubud are the best minds who not only practise and perform culturally and academically accepted forms in "standard" manner but also can create new forms of equal magnitude. The usual complaint that the musical standard, for that matter the performances made for tourists, in Bali naturally has gone down since so many groups perform for foreigners is "open to question and difficult to generalize about" (Tenzer 1991: 25). Performances made for the tourists in Ubud are art created and disseminated by the best minds engaged in the making of the world of the Balinese performing art and culture. And, art by its nature is not only "notoriously hard to talk about" but also "unnecessary to do so" (Geertz 1983: 94) as there are always "inconsistencies, spontaneity, and unpredictability in behaviour in the arts," and such nature of art makes us realize the "mystery, imagination, and the unfathomable creative impulse" (Throsby 1994: 4) and this is how the "artworld" thrives everywhere and at all times. Thus to assume that tourists everywhere come to watch unauthentic, "touristic" performances is to tread upon slippery ground.

Similarly, the culture of performing for tourists is not an act of Westernizing the Balinese performance culture but is part of the logic put by scholars like Samuel Huntington that modernization "does not necessarily mean Westernization" but can be an act of strengthening the culture that "reduces the relative power of the West" (Huntington 1996: 78). By performing ritualistic as well as entertaining dance and drama forms for the tourists, the performers or the "artworlders" in Ubud perform a knowledge and skill of lifting ritual "from its original setting" and perform them as theatre (Schechner 1983: 150-51). Also by performing several versions of the traditional and religious dance to tourists, they act out the logic that the meaning of original art form lies in multiple forms that it can give to. Importantly, by doing so the performers in Ubud learn to represent their art, culture and themselves to the world outside in the context of globalization. Not to perform for tourists, a profession that they have given continuity to almost a century now, is to accept the hegemony that the locals especially of the "Third World" countries cannot or do not know how to represent their art and culture in the context of globalization. Thus by performing for the tourists, artists from Ubud also assert the power and the importance of being "critical" locals, not mere "apolitical creatures" but someone who can generate art, wisdom and skills that are very essential to manage performance culture in newer socio-economic and cultural context.

The performance culture that has come to function in Ubud these days can also be taken as a counter argument against the "inter" and "intra"-cultural theatrical experimentations that have taken place in the West and the post-colonial East respectively for almost one hundred years. Balinese dance and drama performed in the *Colonial Exposition* in 1931 in Paris for the first time in the West was watched by Antonine Artaud, one of the pioneers and the *gurus* of the cross-cultural experimentations in Western theatre. But ironically, the "children" of the same performers whose performances were watched in Paris by Artaud have created a history or reality that local performing arts need not necessarily be taken as a source for cross-cultural experimentation or intra-cultural modern, post-modern, Western and post-colonial Eastern theatrics only but can also be performed and practised as they "are" in their plural forms: traditional, modern and contemporary. There are sixty performances made for the tourists in a week in Ubud. Several dance and drama forms, of new and traditional types are staged on a daily basis. Ubud as a zone of culture of performing for tourists has also become a zone of learning, experimenting and disseminating great many classical, modern and contemporary Balinese dance and drama forms, and has become a geo-cultural space that proves that cultural art forms can survive and flourish in the age of globalization.

Performers and Tourists

"Legong" and "Barong" have 70 members whereas "Kecak" has at least 150 members in each. Average number of the audience that most of such groups manage to get on a regular basis remains far below the number of their members. Most of the groups perform for tourists once a week only. Performers who manage to perform for more than one group draw some US $ 50 a month. Such formalistic feature of the performing groups for tourists, as far as my research revealed to me, is that virtually not a single performing artist can make a livelihood by the profession of performing for tourists in Ubud alone. Therefore, most of the professional artists combine the profession of performing for tourists in Ubud with other modes of earning. They told the researcher that only performing abroad and carrying out collaborative works with artists from abroad can bring some changes in their lifestyles.

As discussed in the fourth and the fifth chapters, most of the groups are run as part of the *banjar* or community oriented or guided activity. Some 10 to 20 per cent of income of the group is donated to the fund that is spent on managing the temple and venue including musical instruments. Members of such groups do not take any money but donate all to the fund set up to manage regular ceremonies and festivals. Groups formed out of non-*banjar* members divide money every six months, on the *Galungan* day, a religiously important occasion that falls twice a year. Members of all sexes and ages get the same amount of money. Performance made for tourists thus is part of social and cultural activities which include: training local children and youths and women to make professionals, share art and skill with amateurs, and to manage temples and communities-building.

Interviews carried out with several leaders of performing groups and artists show that those who perform for tourists also believe that they make good use of their leisure times. Most of the performers have jobs and run shops during the day throughout the week. The day of performing for the tourists allows them to close or leave the shops earlier in the evening. Performers of the particular day put on traditional dress and come to the temple and meet each other, i.e. practise the social relationship along with the routined performing for tourists. Thus the Turnerian discourse of "freedom from" mundane or routined activities and "freedom to" (Turner 1982: 36-37) create art applies both for tourists as well as performers. Both of the parties free themselves from their routined works for a while, and feel and take part in playing with art as a recreational activity (see *fig.* 24). The performance made for tourists in Ubud enables the locals to act out some "brief moments of freedom and an escape from the daily grind of social responsibilities" (Preston-Whyte 2004: 350). Performances made for tourists, thus enable both performers and audience to live through a moment of recreation.

The performance culture that one can come across in Ubud can be taken as more than a mere practice of performing Balinese dance and drama forms for the tourists. Ubud as a cultural-tourism site reveals out the exigency of creating similar sites through the very medium of performing dance and musical forms of arts of cultural nature to tourists across communities in Asia, especially in Nepal and India where the performance culture of the traditional order is supposed to be in the critical state. Such an attempt can enable the custodians of the performance culture of such nature to create not only a strong base for cultural tourism but importantly also to perform newer roles for themselves. The custodians of such performance cultures too need to learn to practise or perform "critical" roles in the continuity and change state of their performance culture in the context of globalization. They need to remain vigilant in protecting, promoting and inventing performance culture through the medium of regular rehearsals and performances to create audience on a regular basis — the subject of the next chapter.

7

Performing for Tourists and Beyond

Exigency of Performing

THE discussion made on the performance culture practised for tourists, in the previous chapters, leads me to conclude here that the achievements made by the custodians of the Balinese performance culture in Ubud need to be taken into consideration. The reasons are: (a) existence and condition of traditional dance, drama and musical forms in several geo-cultural spaces throughout the world, (b) emergence of the eco-culture of tourism, and (c) exigency of managing and performing knowledge and skills of traditional dance and drama forms in the state of continuity and change. Moreover, the Asian countries share not only similar traditional art forms of the older days but also the reality of the times when transformations are taking place in such art forms because of the cross-cultural movements of people, especially those of the tourists in the present times. In the first section of this chapter, I try to point out a need to redefine tourists, traditional art forms and their practitioners. In the remaining part, I try to problematize the Newar performance culture of the Valley in the changed socio-political state of Nepal in brief. I argue that the artists, cultural and tourism policy makers and custodians of the Kathmandu's performance cultures need to come together and perform both "activism" as well as "aestheticism" to address the traditional Newar performance culture in a changed Nepali political and social context not only to stage them for tourists but importantly to enhance a secure future for such art forms.

Redefining Tourists, Performances and Artists

As discussed in the earlier chapter, the very politics of canonizing performances made for tourists as mere "touristic" which is not a subject of serious attention is always and already deconstructed as the talents or creative minds start to participate in the making of a culture of performing for tourists. The hegemonized forms that the academy, bureaucracy, researchers, the locals and the tourists do promulgate about the performances made for tourists is problematic because it is assumed that such shows can never be authentic. It makes one believe that performances made for tourists as static forms are supposed to remain "below" the standard and against the traditions or cultural ethics and values. But questions are in order: should a performance be regarded as unauthentic simply because it is being watched by tourists? Or should the performance be interpreted or judged by the talents who are involved in making it?

Importantly, the sphere of the audience of traditional dance and drama forms practised in any particular community naturally expands especially at a time and context when we believe that "the local" is a leaky, contingent construction, where "global forces are taken up, struggled over, and refracted for site-specific purposes" (Conquergood, 2008: 369). One is also aware of the fact that the line between "who is a local and who is tourist is not the same as between musicians and non-musicians, or professionals and non-professionals. . . . The locals are the people who, if music were to vanish, would not know what to do" (Fisk, 1998: 208). Therefore, old binaries such as local vs. tourist audience, authentic vs. touristic performance, and performer vs. patron need to be problematized in order to redefine performance, performers and audience of the shows staged for tourists.

Traditional dance and drama forms can flourish and survive in their multiple forms not only of the faith and religion of the people associated with them, but importantly also of the involvement of the individual talents and minds which seek for inventions and interventions from within. They in this part of the world especially in Nepal and India have always been taken as part and parcel of the Indic metaphysics as well as metaphors of some shared grand religious faiths and cultural connections among different cultural communities. It is argued, "To push the point further; it is obvious that there is religion *in* the performing arts of India: the ageless mythology, as well as their references to religious paths towards ultimate spiritual goals, have formed the narrative, structural, and teleological goals of the music, dance and drama since ancient times" (Schwartz, 2004: 3). Therefore, myths, legendary tales and lore attached with traditional or classical dance and drama rather than the very forms, the subject of the aesthetic transformation, have occupied the minds of the cultural policy makers.

But artists everywhere are aware of the socio-cultural and aesthetic context of their times and the need to address it accordingly. They hold power to define or give form and dimension to their art forms according to the audience that they think they mainly work for. Many contemporary Indian dance creators are aware of the fact that a major shift has taken place in the audience structure of their times. Pallavi Chakrovarty highlighting this very issue analyses the spirit of the works of Kumudini Lakhia, a trendsetter contemporary Indian dancer, in the following manner:

> For Kumudini Lakhia, innovation in dance means an intellectual quest for making it relevant to the middle class. She and others like her have been the avant-garde choreographers of the last two decades. They were looking for artistic interaction, informed criticism, a new audience and a new kind of patronage for their works (2008: 159).

Kings and patrons rather than the performers themselves have often been taken as the important source and medium of transformation and preservation of traditional or classical performing arts and cultures by historians and bureaucrats in this part of the world especially in Nepal and India for a long time. In the Kathmandu Valley, a great number of dances are performed for one or the other deity throughout the year, and many of them are supposed to have originated in one or the other king's reign. But families of the artists responsible for conducting such performances have often remained incognito. Chakradhar Sharma, whose forefather is supposed to have created dances for the Newar king of Patan, one of the kingdoms of the Kathmandu Valley of the past, and someone whose family's member still performs the same dance on culturally assigned dates, pleads that a great heritage of performance culture is going to disappear as it has not got any sphere of dissemination (Sharma, 1125 (NS): Introduction). Individual artists have always remained as the very medium through which traditional performing arts have survived for ages. But the culture of defining traditional dance, drama and musical forms according to the Śāstras or canons that academics, elites and bureaucrats, therefore, the nation-state has promulgated, has overshadowed the contribution that the "worlders" of traditional performance culture have made in expanding the very sphere over a long period. Therefore, a culture of recognising the power of individual performers or talents who have given continuity to such art forms through invention and intervention from within needs to be given a greater importance in new social, cultural and academic contexts.

Individual talents in this region, especially in India, such as E. Krishna Ayyar, Uday Shankar, Birju Maharaj, Kumudini Lakhiya, Bandana Sen, Rukmini Devi, Nati Binodini and Shiva Ram Hegade among others have already carved out the heritage of expanding the very sphere of traditional performing arts and culture. Matthew argues that moving classical dance quite deliberately out of the temple to what the dancers felt would be a more respectable home on the secular stage in India, made the dancers and programme presenters feel that the new stage needed some type of spiritual resonance (1998: 19). Similarly, Avanthi Meduri highlighting the contribution made by Rukmini Devi to the world of traditional performance culture in India argues, "To rescue a temple dance, under the threat of disappearance in the 1930s, Rukmini Devi projected a modern temple stage and offered it as an alternative allegorical structure to rescue the dance" (2008: 152). Many individual talents have worked on the footprints of Devi and others in contemporary times in India and Nepal.

Traditional dance and drama forms in India, especially in Kerala have gone through greater modes of transformations in contemporary times. They have been taken as the source of energy for modern theatrics in Kerala, for that matter in India. Kerala has become "a cookie jar for those interested in the performing arts", and many art forms have survived and done well "despite the total collapse of the feudal patronage structure" and "the enormous social changes that took place during the twentieth century" (Daugherty, 2000: 3, 5). The Kerala-based dance and drama forms have become the source of intercultural theatrics for both Indian as well as non-Indian theatre creators from Europe and America. They have also been interpreted into new forms that reflect the changing social and aesthetic values of Kerala, India. They are still being performed as part of temple festivals and ceremonies, and are often taken as a possible strong medium of vibrant tourism culture. Similarly, Kavalam Narayan Panikkar is often credited for giving a new lease of life to the ages-old Sanskrit theatrics in our times. It is reviewed that Panikkar's creations have themes in close proximity to real life, its anxieties, struggles and confusion:

> Panikkar thus brought a classic more than 1,500 years old within the reach of the masses who responded to it enthusiastically. Though Panikkar is accused of following an eclectic approach, all these elements were integrated to create a harmonious, highly pleasing performance.
>
> (Kothari and Panchal, 1984: 112-13)

Evoking the creative roles that the individual talents have played by giving dynamism to the traditional performance culture in the post-colonial context of India, Kapila Vatsyayan writes,

> The storehouse was so rich and the layer of dust so weak that the sincere artiste had only to dig a little to discover its essential luminosity. During the past five decades, many layers of past artistic glory have been uncovered. The digging continues and each time one delves deeper, a greater treasure is discovered. (1997: 8)

Therefore, there is a strong need to recognize the power or the value of the "diggers" who visit the "archaeology sites" of the traditional art forms as conscious or "critical" talents and interpret the heritage as an "ever present arena" not a thing of the past. Importantly, while doing it, the "diggers" have affirmed an identity that they are most responsible inhabitants of the world of the traditional performance culture and arts of an important order, not mere practitioners of a task given by the people living in the upper echelon of the traditional societies.

Thus it is high time that one made a counter discourse to the ones that regard the South Asian traditional dance and drama forms as a collective noun and repeat the same grand narratives about it. The important thing is to trace down the cultural site where specific art form is going through the process of transformation because of the involvement of the individual artist. Such an exercise will help us to celebrate and enhance the very power that an individual creative and critical mind holds to give dynamism to the traditional art forms. Chakravorty pointing out the very fact that an individual artist can be an important intellectual carving out new discourse and modes of expression in the very world of art that he or she does practise in, writes,

> Kumudini Lakhia and others were able to go beyond the *gharānās* and reclaim classical dance in general as a form of individual self-expression. The idea of choreography is thus tied to the notion of individual self-expression and authorship. This shift in Indian dance also reflects the changing patronage of dance in India — from predominately the state to private organizations and a new network of global sponsors. (2008: 149)

To borrow words from Vatsyayan, Lakhiya is a "digger" motivated by energy of the new age and demand.

But Why Tourism?

Since traditional performance arts have always remained in the "continuity and change " state of their own, and individual talents have always brought intervention and invention from within, why does then one need to wait for tourists to arrive in his or her community. I think the transformation that the Balinese performance culture has managed to go through (as discussed in the earlier chapters) provides answers to it. Tourism has become an important future course for the traditional performance cultures and arts in South Asia especially in India and Nepal. For example, the government and accommodation industry are projecting the state (Kerala) as a major tourist attraction (Sreekumar and Parayil, 2002: 530). The process appears to be the same in the Kathmandu Valley as well. Tourism policies of both places regard tourism business as a source of opportunities that the practitioners of the local performance culture or traditional dance and drama forms can draw from. Regarding this issue of cultural policies that local as well as national bodies need to develop especially in a time and place where cultural tourism is supposed to be the main source of income and mode of lives, T.C. Chang and W.K. Lee write,

> . . . the provision of physical *hardware* must be complemented with the cultivation of a creative *heartware* — spaces sensitively customized for the arts and accompanying policy mindsets that appreciate the arts for their intrinsic rather than economic value. A balance between the instrumentalist and humanistic vision of the arts ought to be struck.
>
> (2003: 139)

Chang and Lee argue that government must not only create and show culturally and artistically important sites to the tourists for the sake of earning money but should also help the artists to create art and culture of a vibrant and fresh nature. Therefore, the performance culture that one comes across in Ubud can be taken as a possible mode of transformation that the traditional dance and drama forms in India and Nepal too can go through.

Traditional Performance Culture in Nepal

Traditional dance, drama and musical forms are rarely practised outside the cultural sites and occasions in Kathmandu metropolis. Therefore, the number of their professional practitioners has always remained a few. Members of the younger generation of the Newar and the non-Newar communities in Kathmandu are unfamiliar with the heritage of the traditional dance and drama forms of the Valley. Most of the ages-old social and cultural organizations and foundations set to manage such art forms have become defunct now. This has created a fear that people soon are going to lose a heritage of an important order. Traditional performing art forms, by the very reason that they are performing arts, can survive only if they are rehearsed and performed on a regular basis. When members of an art community form a group and decide to perform their traditional dance, drama and musical forms on a regular basis, they take part in the process of rehearsing, i.e. creating new forms and discourses and give continuation to the heritage in a very pragmatic manner. They feel pressurized for staging their art forms not in a mono-aesthetic style but in multiple forms. While doing this, they take an important adventure of exploring the domain of their art, culture and profession through inventing, discovering and reinterpreting traditional dance and drama forms in a new order. Only this culture of engaging or "digging" within can provide a new dynamism to the traditional performing culture. When practitioners themselves set on a journey of the above kind then only do they feel secure about their future, and expand and extend the very domain that they work for and have lived with for ages.

The first meeting of the constituent assembly declared Nepal as a republic nation on 28 May 2008. Political protagonists of different generations and ideological backgrounds are working on the scripts of a nation of the republican textures. Will these phenomenal tremors in politics and emotions of Nepalis bring any changes in their traditional performance culture? What will happen to the roles performed by the king as the head of state on the cultural events and performances in Nepal, especially in the Kathmandu Valley since many cultural performances demanded the ceremonial presence of the "king"? Are traditional communities and committees formed to look after such cultural events and performances prepared to explore out alternatives? Will the absence of the "king" as protagonist make any difference for such performances?

But the political history of Nepal shows that the traditional performing art and culture of the Valley has suffered a lot because of insensitive and avaricious nature of some members of the ruling class family and clans. Many sculptures and icons of great aesthetics, cultural and spiritual faiths started to disappear during the regime when the monarchy enjoyed its heyday in Nepal. Historians and researchers have pointed out that many traditional cultural committees such as *guthi* and *mahābihāra*s among others formed for conducting traditional dance, drama and cultural performances faced hard times as the resources which such committees functioned with were overtaken by the members of the ruling class families. Palaces of the Shahs and the Ranas, the families of the former rulers of Nepal, stood on the land that was supposed to provide the resources that many cultural organizations and committees once functioned with. Many of them have now been turned into private hotels and governmental offices but the traditional performance culture and the social organizations concerned have remained poor and defunct.

Moreover, traditional performance culture has survived and flourished in many republican states. Its situation in Bali (Indonesia) and India reveals to us that republican state and traditional performance culture are not binary entities. Many Indian and Balinese dance and drama forms which were

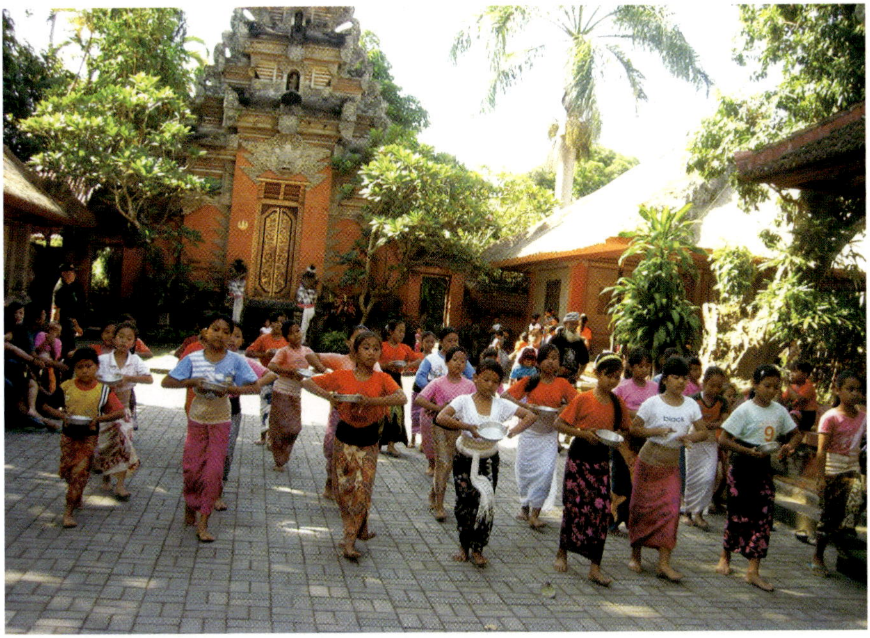

fig. 1. Seen in the picture are local kids learning dances in Sanggar in the Puri Ubud.

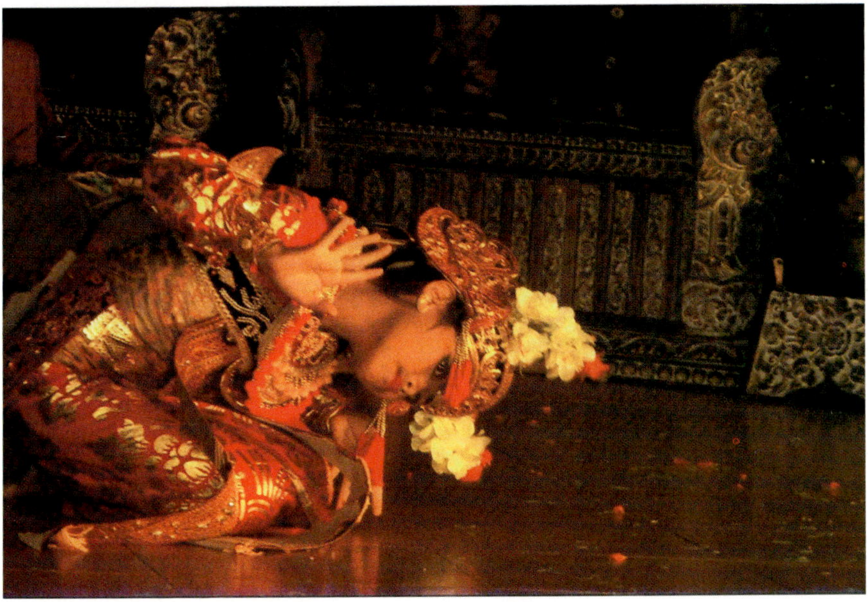

fig. 2. Seen in the picture is a nine year-old-girl artist performing for the tourists. She belongs to a group called Nirtta Dewi.

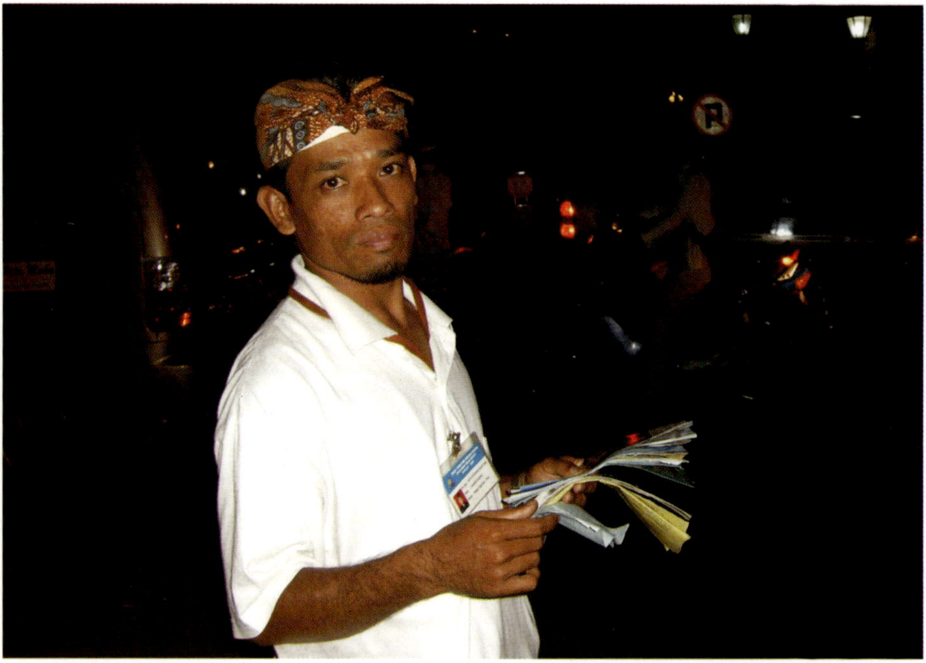

fig. 3. Seen in the picture is a ticket seller waiting for tourists to approach him near the courtyard of the Puri Ubud.

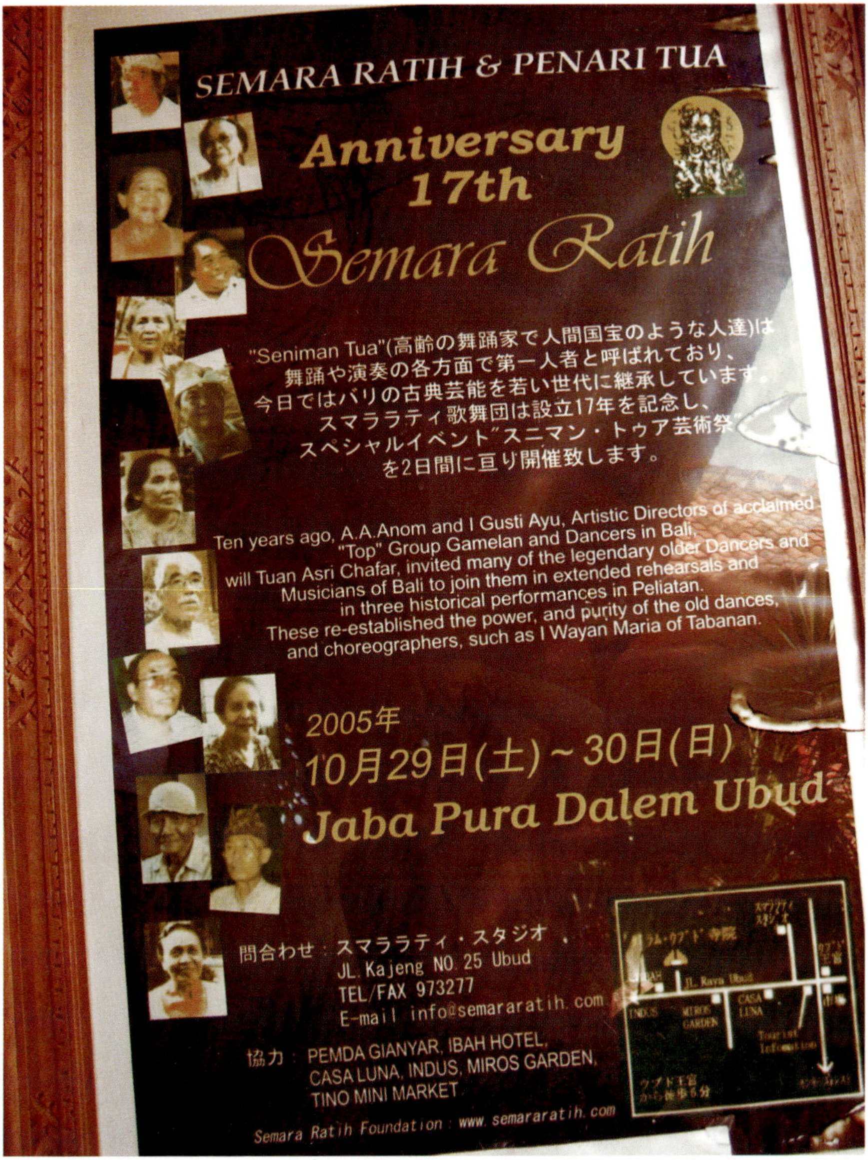

fig. 4. Audiences in most of the venues are welcomed and bid farewell in Japanese as well as English languages.

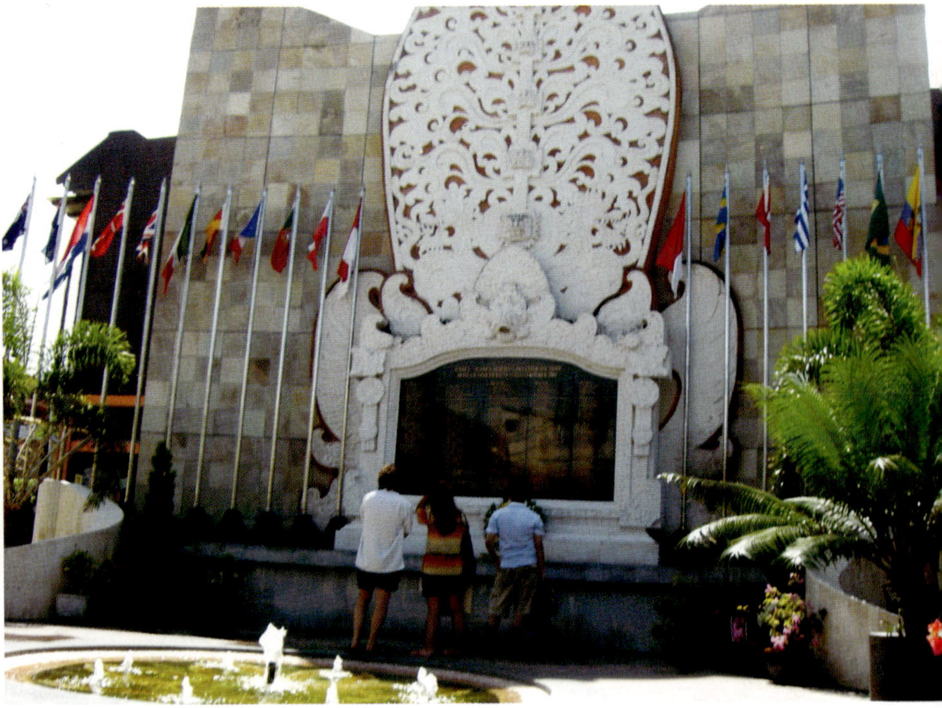

fig. 5. Seen in the picture is the monument erected in the memory of those killed in the 2002 Bali Bombing in Kuta.

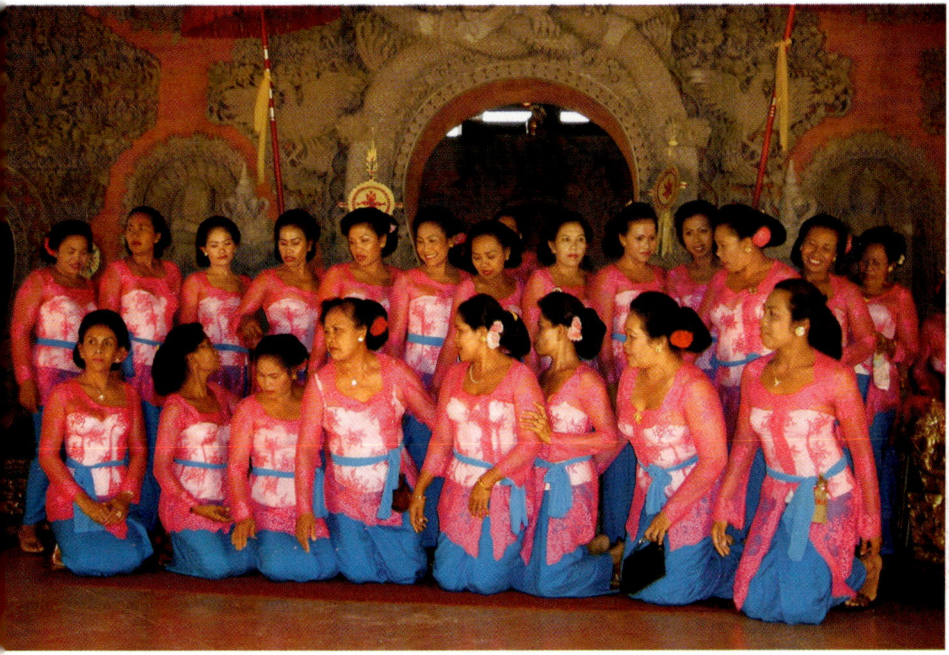

fig. 6. Seen in the picture is a recently formed women's gamelan group from Ubud.
I frequently visited the rehearsal that the group went through.
After the ritual of mesakapan — the marriage ceremony
between the musical instruments and performers,
the group is about to stage their creation
for the representatives from the LISTIBIYA
and local custodians of
dance and drama forms.

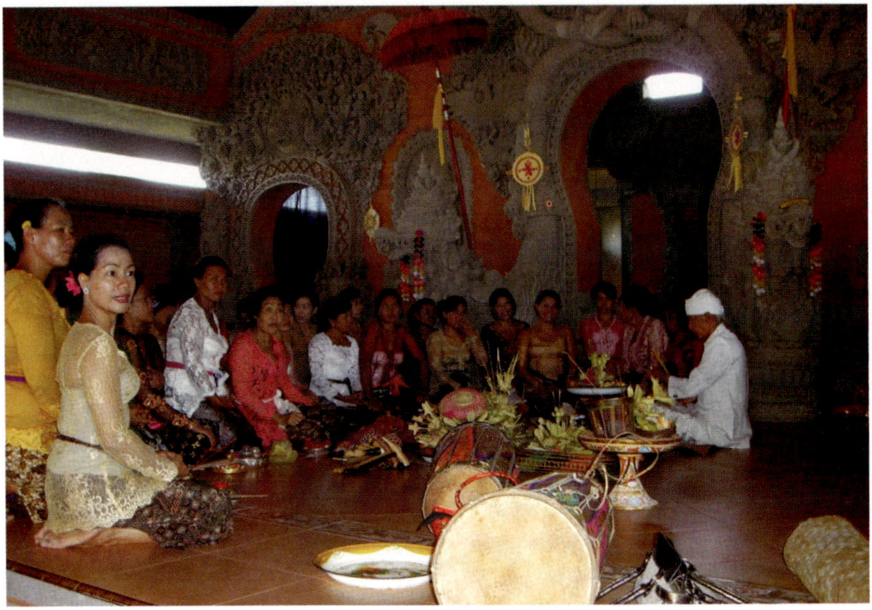

fig. 7. Seen in the picture is a scene of mesakapan, a ritual performed to mark the marriage between musical instruments and musicians or performers.

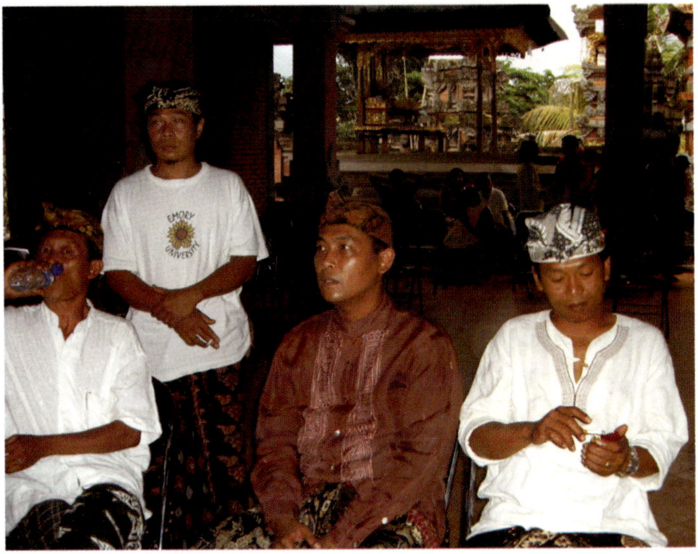

fig. 8. Seen in the picture are Tjokorda Ngurah Suyadnya (second from the right), Wakil Legislatif from the Puri Saraswati Ubud, the representative of the LISTIBIYA and the music instructor Swastika Raka (the first from the left) watchingthe performance of the newly formed women's gamelan.

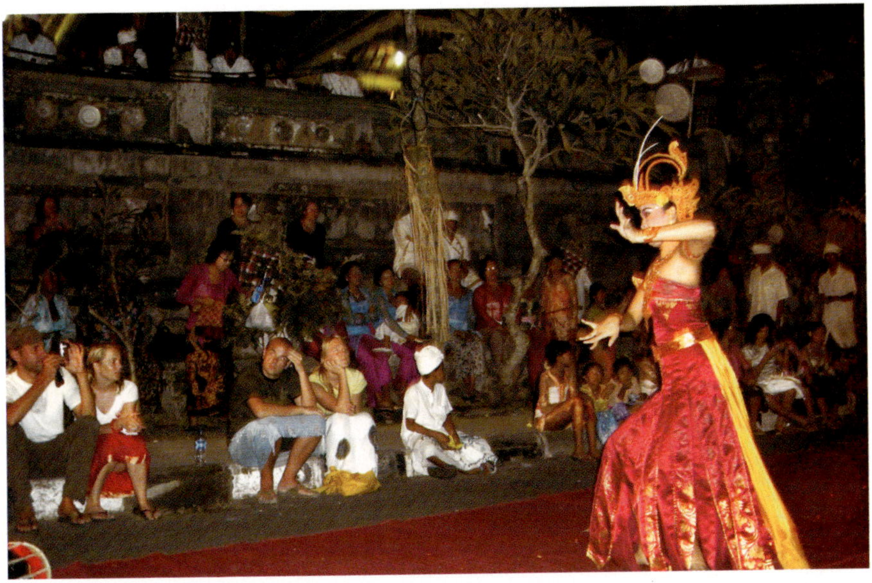

fig. 9. On the occasions of temple ceremonies, local, tourists and expats gather to watch the same performance that the tourists watch on a regular basis in Ubud.

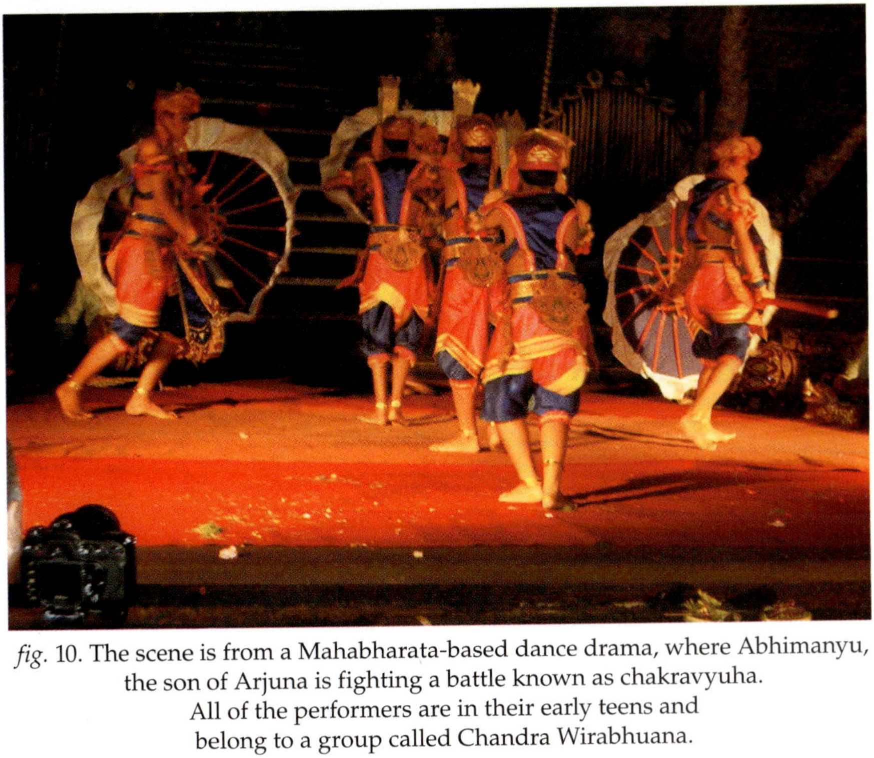

fig. 10. The scene is from a Mahabharata-based dance drama, where Abhimanyu, the son of Arjuna is fighting a battle known as chakravyuha. All of the performers are in their early teens and belong to a group called Chandra Wirabhuana.

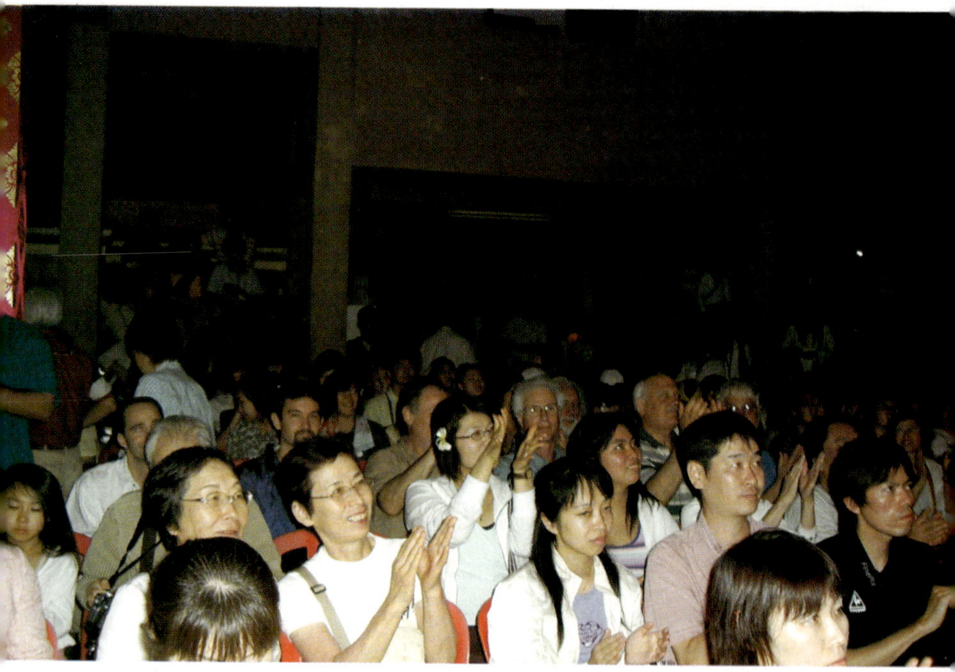

fig. 11. In the recent years, Japanese tourists have become the most visible audience of the performance culture in Ubud.

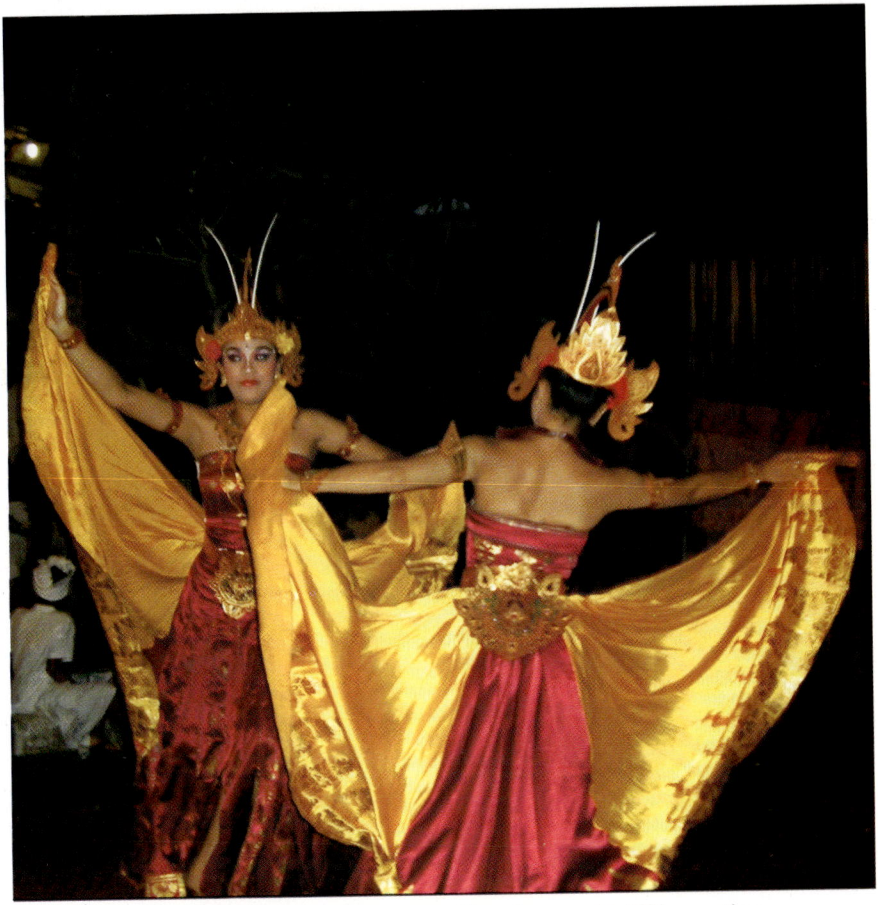

fig. 12. This dance is known as Chandrawarshi, ISI's creation and is one of the most performed pieces for the tourists in Ubud.

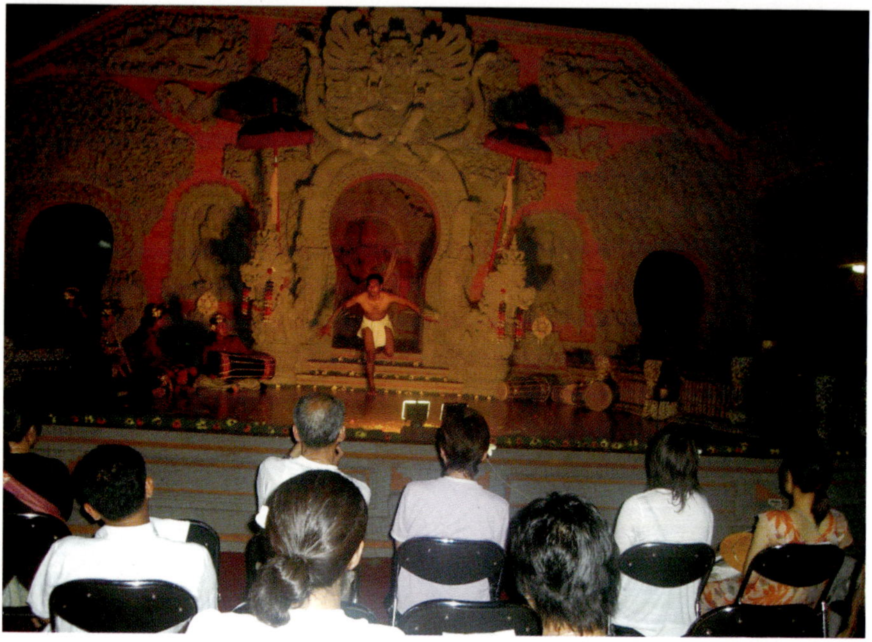

fig. 13. Seen in the picture is a contemporary creation of the group called Nirtta Dewi.

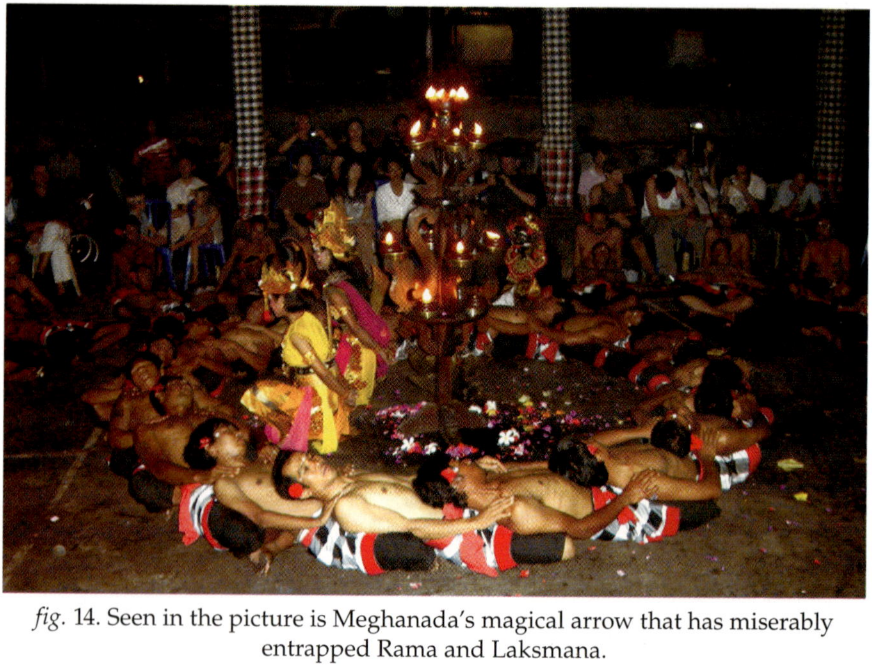

fig. 14. Seen in the picture is Meghanada's magical arrow that has miserably entrapped Rama and Laksmana.

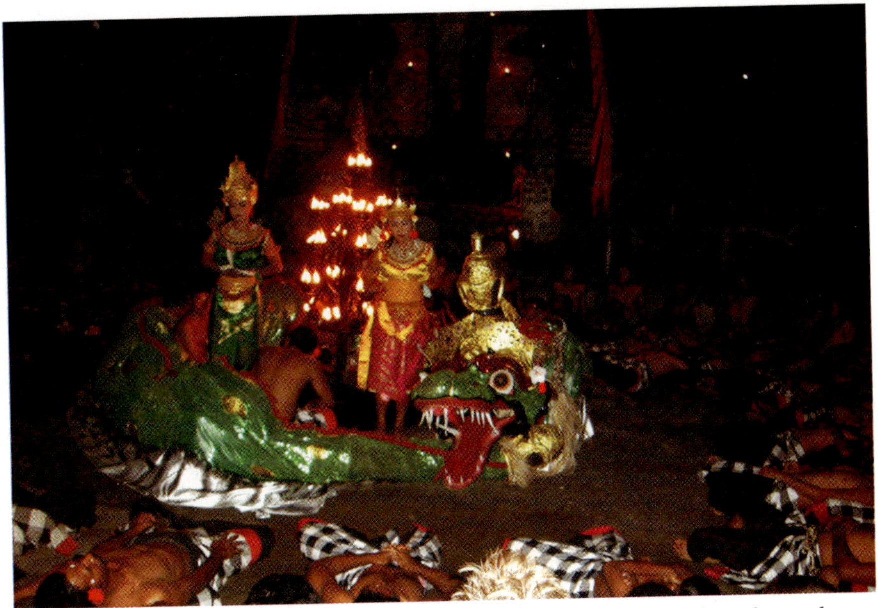

fig. 15. Seen in the picture is a 'naturalistic' dragon used and performed to depict the war between Rawana and Rama by the Cecak group from Jungjugan village.

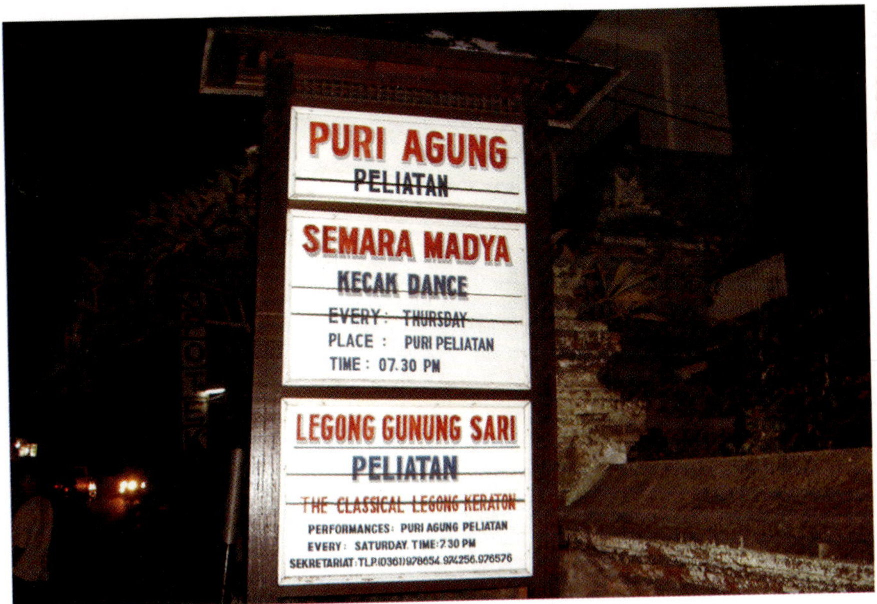

fig. 16. Seen in the board is the schedule of performances for tourists in Puri Agung in Peliatan.

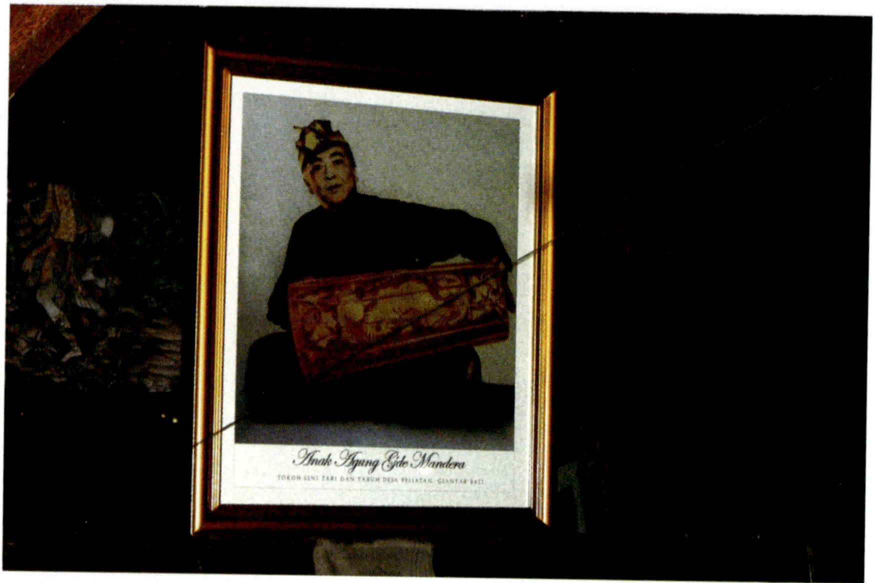

fig. 17. Seen in the picture is a photo of the late Agung Mandera, the man who played an important role in carving out identity for dance and music in Peliatan style.

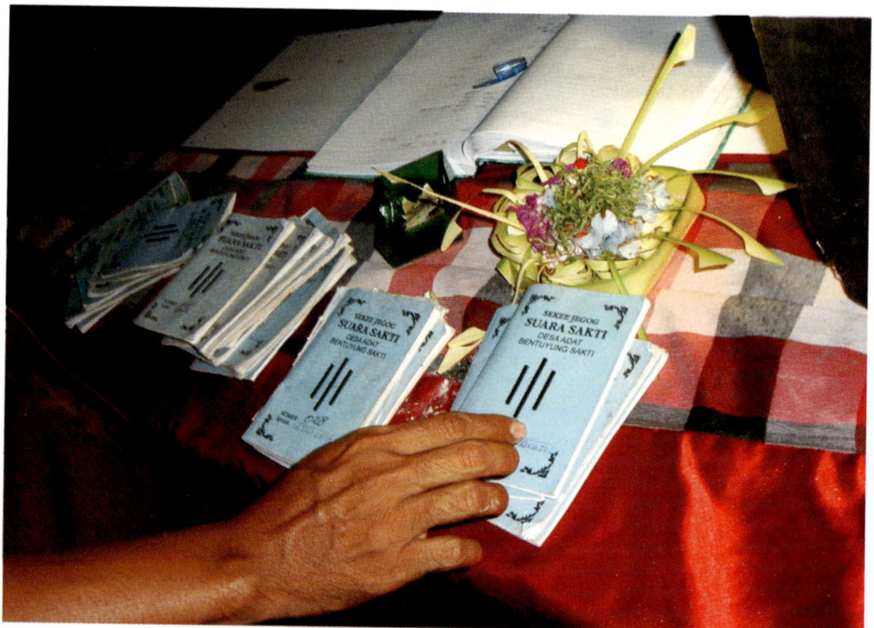

fig. 18. Seen in the picture are identity cards of the members of the group. The card contains records of his or her attendance and earning.

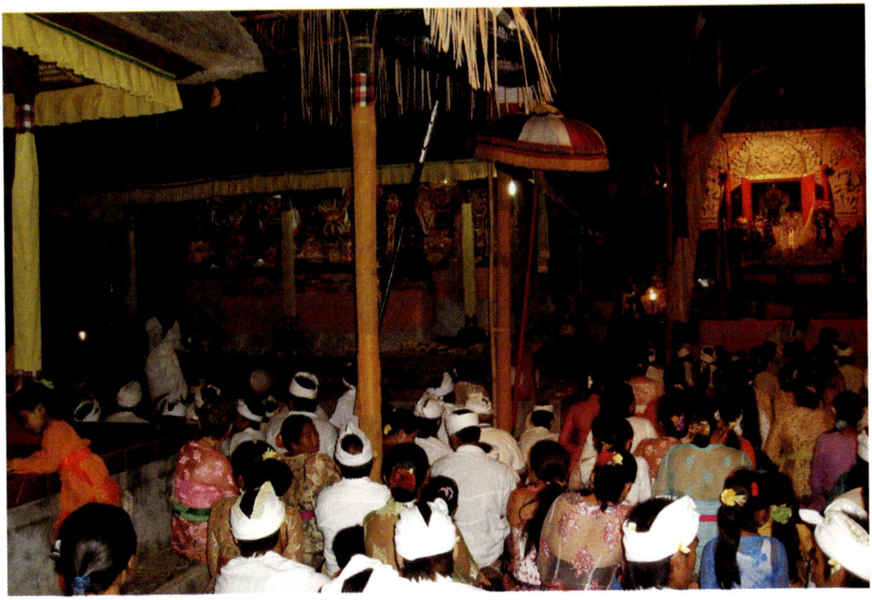

fig. 19. In the recent years, ceremonies in Ubud have become more spectacular. Most of the performing groups contribute major part of their income to certain temple as well as to the community funds that are spent for buying paraphernalia that are required for conducting ceremonies.

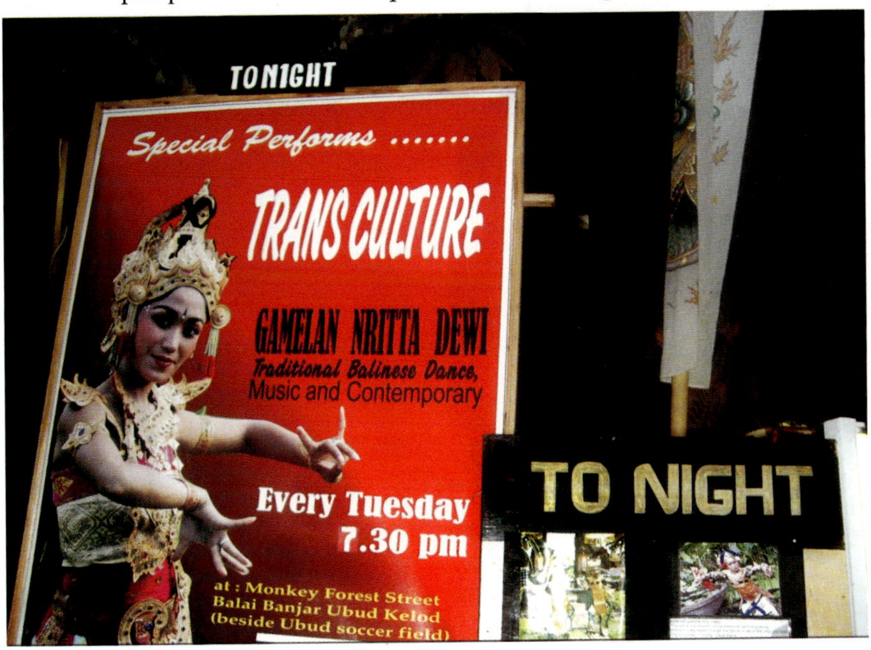

fig. 20. Seen in the picture is a board mentioning about the schedule for performance put in front of the Banjar building in the Monkey Forest area.

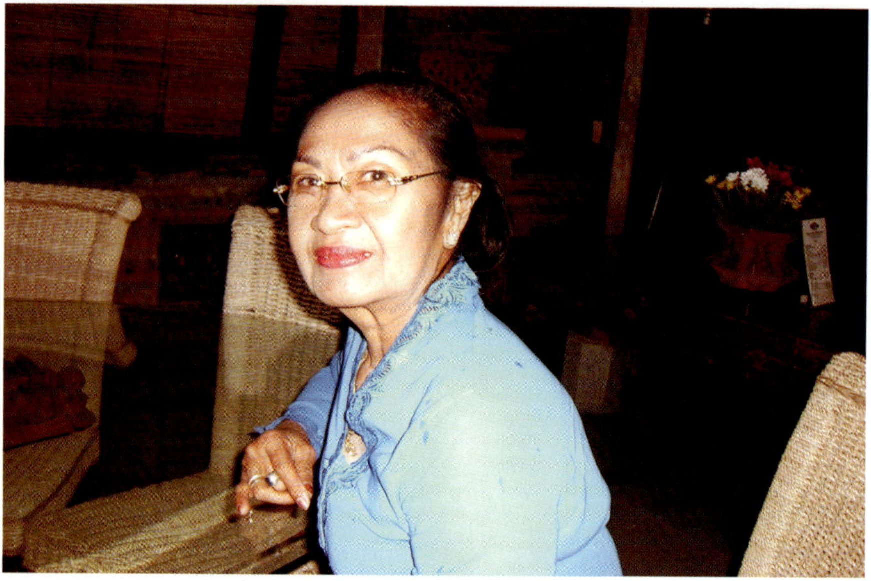

fig. 21. Seen in the picture is Raka Rashmi who was trained by the late Mario. She is in her seventies and teaches dance to children from the local communities in the Arma Museum, Pangosekan.

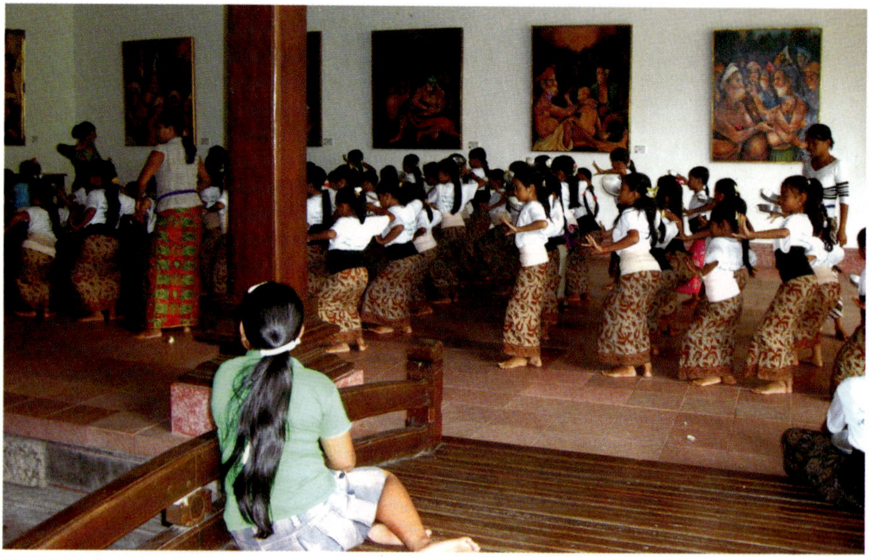

fig. 22.Seen in the picture are local children learning dances in the Arma Museum. At the far corner is seen Raka Rasmi, someone who was trained by the late Mario, the genius, who is supposed to have given the Kebyar phenomenon a greater magnitude.

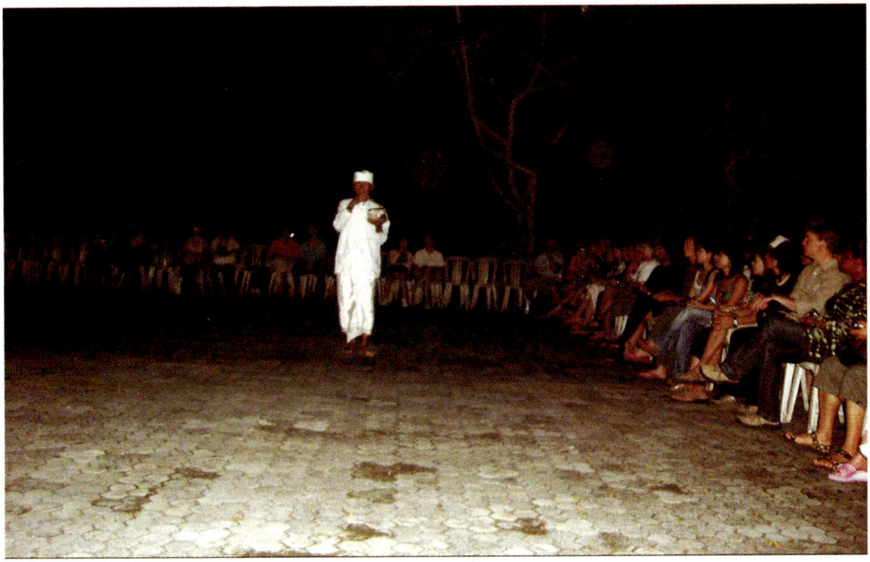

fig. 23. A local priest is purifying the venue before the performers appear on the stage.

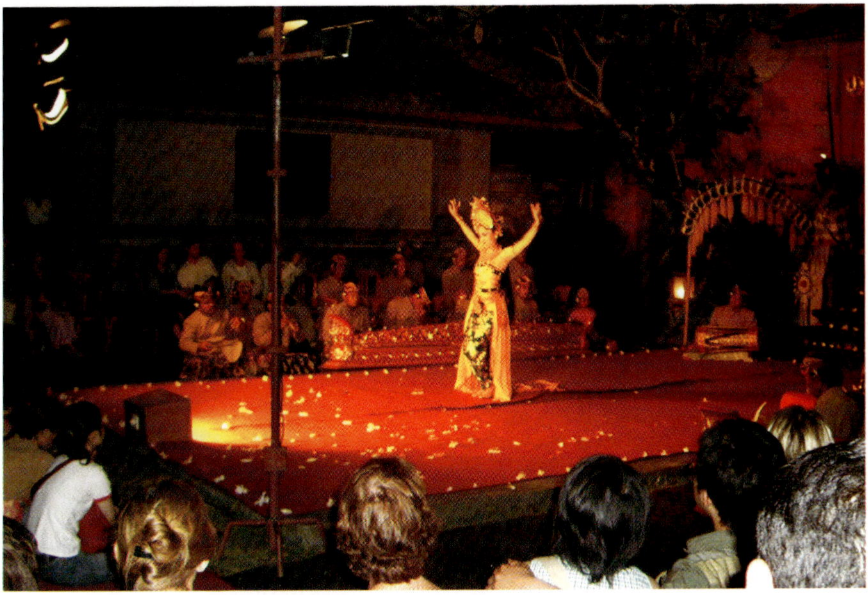

fig. 24. Seen in the picture is a moment when audiences find themselves intensely watching a performance.

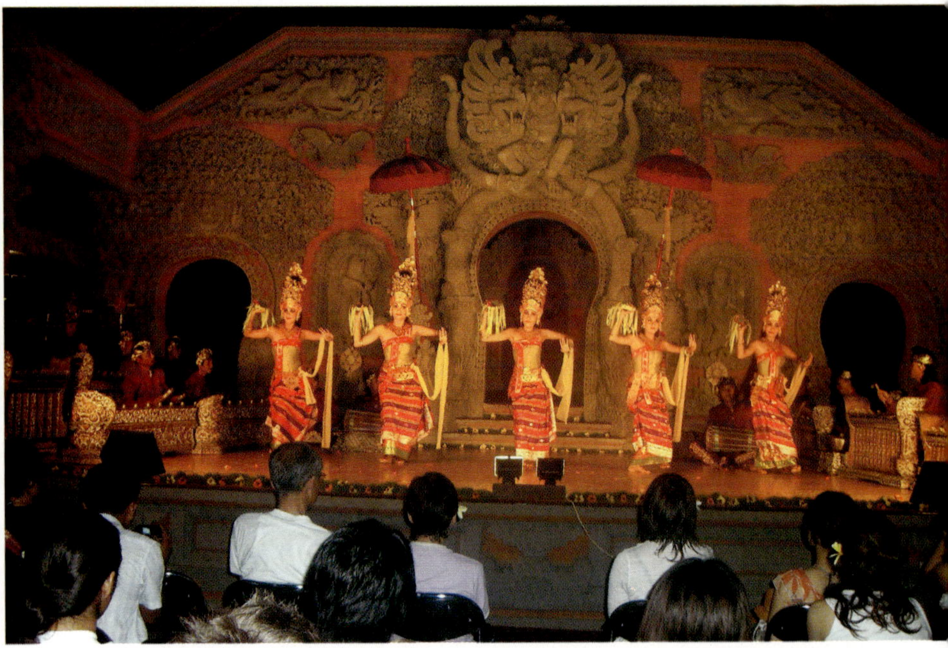

fig. 25.Seen in the picture is the magnificent stage inside the Banjar building at the Monkey Forest Area, and artists performing 'welcome dance' to their audiences, the tourists.

invented in the palace to entertain kings have seen better days as they are performed regularly these days, and importantly, performers and audience themselves have become the patrons of such arts in the changed cultural context of our times. Similarly, dance and drama which dramatize the story of kings and his lovers do not make the performance feudalistic. Traditional performing arts too keep on changing their semiotics and stylistics as their audience experiences the political and cultural transformations that their societies go through.

Therefore, the members of cultural communities and committees such as *guthi* and *mahābihāra* among others in the Kathmandu Valley, Nepal need to come up with alternate modes of performing their responsibilities. Traditional mode of managing cultural events and performances in Kathmandu needs to be given a new transformation since there is a need of purging traditional performance culture off its feudalistic and undemocratic mind set. Local performers, no matter how glocal the society they belong to, may be the last bastions of the traditional performance art and cultures. They are the sole protectors of their dance and drama forms. Cultural policy makers and academicians everywhere must realize a fact that traditional performance culture can thrive only when its custodians come together and construct the membership of their communities democratically and feel a pleasure as well as need and pride of performing their age-old art. Heads of the states keep on coming and going but the show must go on.

The pasts offer creative challenges to us in every bend of peoples' lives, and that of the nation for that matter. Temples, palaces, monasteries, and public spaces in the Kathmandu Valley represent important memories associated with the bygone eras. They stand tall sending shadows or ripples over the minds of the visitors, tourists, artists and dreamers. Associated with them are the art forms and the aesthetics of the former days. But the important thing at present is to accept the challenges of the very art and aesthetics created in the past times. The challenge would mean to create similar monuments and write texts that would speak of our aspirations to move beyond the canons and cultures set by the older regimes and cultural systems. The important thing is not to erase the beautiful shadows of imagination that the people in the past lived and worked with, but move ahead with genuine dreams of creating greater, more magnificent temples, monasteries and public spaces in the present times. One can give colour and carve out gods and goddesses to articulate new minds and aspirations. It is not only we human beings but also the gods love going through transformations. Plural and flexible are the deities too. They love to be performed in multiple forms and manners. They are highly performative creatures.

A culturally rich Kathmandu Valley has remained the capital of several nation states of different magnitudes for millennia. Much longer are the histories of its arts and cultures than its political times. Myriads of images that we see in Kathmandu pull us back to its pasts, to the physical and metaphysical trails that this metropolis has marched so far. Such images have always remained here under multiple threats. They have survived not only the sun and the rain but also many natural disasters, political transformations, and suffered public negligence and exploitations. Can a future Kathmandu remain a friendly place to its cultural images, locations and forms? Moreover, can a future Kathmandu evoke the semiotics and semantics of its past while offering opportunities and prosperity to those who come or are here in pursuit of their dreams? What could be the effective strategies of future course to keep the Newar performing arts and cultures vibrant in Nepal of tomorrow?

Urbanization has become a global or universal social and cultural experience. Villages where traditional dance and drama forms once were popular and practised have become towns or are in the process of becoming urban zones, many of which have already become slum areas. Therefore, there is a need to free minds from the belief that traditional art and culture can only exist in village, and it could exist only in the past. Culturally, we belong to the era of globalization, when it is argued that ethnicity can be created and traditional dance and drama forms can be invented and practised. Culture either Western or Eastern, modern or traditional, needs to be taken in its plural forms. Same traditional dance, drama and musical forms can be or are practised in different styles across the communities. Its practitioners also borrow styles, ideas and work accordingly. They also begin their careers as amateurs and gradually achieve a quality of professionals after years of training and performances. Some practitioners always remain better and more dynamic than the others. Some create and practise in newer styles whereas others stop performing in no time. World of traditional performing art too functions and flourishes through the talents of the minds involved in it. Therefore, much depends on the quality of the minds of the "worlders" of the traditional dance, drama and musical forms too.

Therefore, performing traditional Newar dance and drama forms to the metropolitan audience either domestic or international tourists can provide newer roles to its custodians. Inventing such a culture would mean enabling performers, community organizations and their members and leaders to redefine themselves, their arts and cultures in a newer context. Since several traditional Newar dance and drama forms are associated with one or the other deities of the Newars, the participation of the Newars remains an important agency in such process of transformation. When local performers themselves participate in selecting venue and forms of dance and drama to present for tourists, they embody and exhibit power and take part in a dialogue with the mega form of globalization or global culture. Moreover, when members of an art community get engaged in exercise of rehearsal, discourse-making, and creating and continuing traditional art forms, they create zones of learning of such art forms for their fellow members of different ages and sexes. As a result, phenomena such as tangible as well as intangible "flow" of traditional wisdom, aesthetics, skill and "vocabulary" of performing art and culture take place.

Thus tourists or metropolitan audience, on the one hand, and traditional performing art and culture, on the other, are not binary opposite entities. Researchers and lovers of Newari culture too have pointed out a unique blend of urban and folk-ness in its performing art and culture. Therefore, there is a need to act in time to save a culture from a catastrophe. There is a need of "critical" locals, for that matter the custodians of the traditional performance arts and culture in a changed social, political and economic aesthetic context in places like the Kathmandu Valley.

Glossary of the Balinese, Bhasa Indonesian and Newari Terms

(Terms of the Newari origin, but not others, have been underlined)

Abhimanyu: the son of Arjuna, the protagonist character from the epic, *Mahābhārata*. He is often taken as a scapegoat.

Adat: local Balinese customary law and institution.

Agem: basic Balinese dance posture with weight on the back leg.

Apsaras: nymph, especially who dance in the court of Indra, the king of the Hindu gods.

Arja: a form of Balinese sung dance-drama.

Arjuna: one of the central characters from the *Mahābhārata*.

Balih-balihan: a term used for the dances staged with the purpose of entertaining people.

Bamboo Gamelan: an ensemble of giant bamboo instruments originated from the West Bali.

Banjar: a governmental as well as customary unit that is responsible for solving issues.

Baris: a single or group dance-drama based on action and mood of the warriors.

Barong: a sacred mask dance performed by two men.

Bebali: a term that refers to the ceremonial dances or dances that are performed in the central courtyard of temple or elsewhere on the occasion of ceremonies.

Berutuk: a ritualistic dance and drama that involves bachelors into rigorous ritual for almost one and a half months.

Bhawana agung: macrocosm, from *bhawan* "cosmos," *agung* "great or unfathomable."

Bhawana alit: microcosm, from *bhawan* "cosmos," *alit* "small."

Bina Wisata: the Ubud Tourist Information Centre, founded in 1981 that is located in front of the Puri Ubud.

Calonarang: an exorcist dance-drama based on the eleventh century story of the widow-witch Rangda.

Celuluk: mask of the witch of a particular kind that is threatening as well as entertaining.

Dalang: the master or the narrator who operates the shadow or puppet theatre.

Desa: a village unit of customary nature.

Devanāgarī: the script of the Sanskrit as well as regional languages of India and Nepal.

Galungan: the main Balinese holiday as well as ceremonies that are held every 210 days, and lasts for ten days.

Gambuh: the classical form of the Balinese dance-drama that is said to be the basis of the great many dramatic forms and music in Bali.

Gamelan: a set of instruments; orchestra.

Genders: usually refers to the metallophones that are played with two round-headed mallets.

Gong: a disk-shaped musical instrument.

Guthi: a traditional organization set with the purpose of managing rituals and festivals by the Newars of the Kathmandu Valley.

Hanumān: one of the protagonist characters from the epic *Rāmāyaṇa*.

Indra: the king of all Hindu gods.

ISI: the Indonesian Arts Institute located at Denpasar.

Janger: type of the Balinese dance where young men and women use call and response songs.

Karmaphala: a Hindu belief that good actions in life herald similar results, from *karma* "action," *phala* "fruit."

Kaurava: the antagonist characters from the epic *Mahābhārata*.

Kebayas: the traditional Balinese attire.

Kebyar: literally it means to "burst open." Aesthetically, it refers to the modern style of the Balinese music and dance, born around 1915.

Kecak: refers to the male characters in the Janger dance as well as to the Kecak chorus whereby a large group of men chant *cak*.

Kṛṣṇa Praṇāmī: a cult within the Hindus in Nepal and India that mainly regards the lord Kṛṣṇa as their main deity and celebrates metaphysics or *līlā* of Kṛṣṇa.

Legong Keraton: a dance form performed by two girls originated in the eighteenth century.

Legong sabas: another variety of dance in Legong form.

Listibia (LISTIBIYA): the Balinese Government Council on the Arts.

Mahābihāras: an organization or the premise where monasteries and temples are located, that looks after the rituals and the ceremonies of the Newar Buddhists of the Kathmandu Valley.

Mesakapan: a ritualistic ceremony conducted with the purpose of marrying musicians with their musical instruments.

Negara: a kingdom or state.

Niṣkala: the invisible world, un-manifested.

Nyepi: the Balinese New Year.

Ogoh-ogoh: effigies produced to be paraded on the eve of the Balinese New Year, and are burnt down next morning.

Oleg Tumulilingan: a dance form created by Mario, and is also known as "Bumble-Bee" dance.

Penasar: those who provide a foundation, buffoon characters serving as attendants to the princess in Balinese theatre.

Pāṇḍava: the five protagonist characters (Yudhiṣṭhira, Bhīma, Arjuna, Nakula and Sahadeva) from the epic *Mahābhārata*.

Pariwisata budaya: the Cultural tourism; in Bali it was developed with the purpose of enabling the Balinese locals to intensify their cultures to attract tourists. It was also stated that the revenues generated by tourism should be used to preserve and promote the cultures in Bali.

Pārvatī: the goddess, as well as, the consort of lord Śiva.

Pedanda: a Balinese priest who presides at a temple ritual.

Pendet: a ritual dance also known as "welcome dance" that is performed to welcome not only tourists or guests but also gods.

Poepoetan: literally "the self-sacrifice." It mainly refers to the historic war that many royalties and commoners from Bali fought against the Dutch Empire in 1906.

Pramana Patram Budaya: the Certificate of Artistic Excellence granted to troupes of Balinese musicians and dancers authorized to perform for foreign audience.

Pura: a temple or sacred space or building from where Balinese can make communication to gods.

Puri: palace, the residence of lord.

Rāma: the Hindu god, or the central protagonist from the epic *Rāmāyaṇa*.

Rangda: a mask of demonic aspect charged with magical power, and is believed to protect the community against epidemics.

Rāvaṇa: the antagonist character, the demon-king, from the epic *Rāmāyaṇa*.

Ṛṣi Mārkaṇḍeya: a sage who is supposed to have set the Hindu civilization in Bali in the eighth century.

Sāī-Bābā: a contemporary religious cult popular among the Hindus of India as well as Nepal that regards Sāī-Bābā, a particular genius as the god-incarnated.

Sanggar: music or dance studio or club that performs as well as teaches or trains youths.

Sanghyang: the exorcistic rites which are characterized by spirit possession executed during epidemics.

Saputs and Udengs: some of the accoutrements that are required for funerary for the Balinese Hindus.

Sarongs: the traditional Balinese attire.

Sekaa: voluntary association; collectives of mutual aid or co-operation organized around specific functions.

Sekala: the visible world, perceived by the senses.

Seni provan: *seni* "art," *provan* "not sacred."

Seni sacral: *seni* "art," *sacral* "sacred."

Seniman alam: artist especially the one who teaches in traditional manner in the local context.

Śāstra: canonical texts that determine meanings in books as well as life.

Śiva: the lord Śiva.

Sītā: the female protagonist from the epic *Rāmāyaṇa*.

Taksu: spiritual charisma of a performer.

Tandang and Tangkis: words which refer to movements or foot step in the Balinese dance.

Tari lepas: "free dances"; dances detached from all ritual or dramatic ties in order to be presented as mere entertainment.

Taruna Jaya: a kind of dance that depicts the moods and actions of a youth in Bali.

Tīrtha yātrā: *Tīrtha* "holy," *yātrā* "pilgrimage." Refers to the pilgrimage that the Balinese Hindus make inside as well as outside Bali.

Tri-hita-kāraṇa: *tri* "three," *hita* "helpful," *kāraṇa* "reasons." Refers to the harmony that needs to be maintained among the human beings, the environment and the creator.

Wali: "sacred dances" performed in the inner courtyard of temple or wherever a ceremony is taking place.

Wayang Kulit: shadow puppet play in which puppets made from buffalo hide and representing characters from stories are cast upon a screen by a performer.

Bibliography

Allen, Matthew Harp, "Rewriting the Script for South Indian Dance", *The Drama Review* (1988) 41.3 (Autumn, 1997): 63-100.

Ashworth, Gregory J. and John E. Tunbridge, "Whose Tourist-Historic City? Localising the Global and Globalizing the Local", *A Companion to Tourism*, eds. Alan A. Lew, C. Michael Hall, and Alan M. Williams, USA: Blackwell Publishing, 2004, 210-22.

Ateljevic, Irena and Stephen Doorne, "Cultural Circuits of Tourism: Commodities, Place, and Re-consumption", *A Companion to Tourism*, eds. Alan A. Lew, C. Michael Hall, and Alan M. Williams. USA: Blackwell Publishing, 2004, 291-302.

Ballinger, Rucina, "Historic Ubud", *Ubud is a Mood*, Directed and designed by Leonard Lueras, Bali: The Bali Purnati Book, 2004. 14-32.

Bandem, Made I., and Fredrik Eugene deBoer, *Balinese Dance in Transition: Kaja and Kelod*, Singapore: Oxford University Press, 1995.

Bandem, Made I., "Kebyar: A Monumental Achievement in Balinese Arts", *Mudra. Special Issue* (2006): 1-21, Denpasar: Indonesian Institute of the Arts (ISI), 2006.

Bandem, Made I., "Traditions of Indonesian Arts and Now", *Mudra. Special Edition* (2004): 16-29, Denpasar: Indonesian Institute of the Arts (ISI), 2004.

Bandem, Swasthi Widjaja N.L.N. "Dissemination of Dance in Societies", *Mudra. Special Edition* (2006): 52-64, Denpasar: Indonesian Institute of the Arts (ISI), 2006.

Bandem, Swasthi Widjaja N.L.N., "Traditional Dance as Source of Creativity", *Mudra. Special Edition* (2004), 59-69, Denpasar: Indonesian Institute of the Arts (ISI), 2004.

Barba, Eugenio, "Cultural Identity and Professional Identity", *The Tradition of ISTA*, FILO, tr. Judy Barba, Leo Sykes, ed. Rina Skeel, Londrina: International Festival of Londrina and Universidade Estadual de Londrina, 1994.

Chakravorty, Pallabi, *Bells of Change: Kathak Dance, Women and Modernity in India*, Kolkata: Seagull Books, 2008.

Chang, T.C., and Shirlena Huang, "Urban Tourism: Between the Local Global and the Local", *A Companion to Tourism*, eds. Alan A. Lew, C. Michael Hall, and Alan M. Williams, USA: Blackwell Publishing, 2004, 223-34.

Chang, T.C. and W.K. Lee, "Renaissance City Singapore: a study of art spaces", *Royal Geographical Society*, 2003: 128-41.

Clara B. Wilpert, Preface: "Paradise Bali?", *Bali Living in Two Worlds*, tr. I. Gusti Raka Panji Tisna, eds. Urs Ramseyer and I Gusti Raka Panji Tisna, Schwabe: Museum der Kulturen, 2001, 7-8.

Clifford, James, "Indigenous Articulation", ed. David Welchman Gegeo, *Culture Rupture and Indigeneity: The Challenge of (Re)visioning "Place" in the Pacific*, Hawai'i: University of Hawai'i Press, 2001. 467-90.

Clune, Frank, and Percy Stephensen, "The Monkey Dance", ed. Adrian Vickers, *Traveling to Bali: Four Hundred Years of Journeys*, Kuala Lumpur: Oxford University Press, 1994, 245-50.

Coast, John, *Dancing out of Bali*, London: Faber and Faber, 1954.

Cody and Lynn Shwaiko, "The Mood of Ubud", *Ubud is a Mood*, Directed and designed by Leonard Lueras, Bali: The Bali Purnati Book, 2004, 33-48.

Cohen, Erik, "The Sociology of Tourism: Approaches, Issues, and Findings", *Annual Review of Sociology*, 10 (1984): 373-92.

Cok Sawitri, "Women Versus Men: A Strife in the Field of the Performing Arts", *Bali Living in two Worlds*, tr. I. Gusti Raka Panji Tisna, eds. Urs Ramseyer and I. Gusti Raka Panji Tisna. Schwabe: Museum der Kulturen, 2001, 129-38.

Conquergood, Dwight, "Performance Studies: Interventions and Radical Research", *The Performance Studies Reader*, ed. Henry Bial, London: Routledge, 2008, 369-80.

Costola, Sergio, "Paris/Artaud/Bali: Antonin Artaud Vede il Teatro Balinese all "Espossizione Coloniale di Parigi del 1931", *Asian Theatre Journal*, 20 (2) Fall 2003: 253-55.

Couperus, Louis, "Doing It in Style", *Traveling to Bali: Four Hundred Years of Journeys*, ed. Adrian Vickers, Kuala Lumpur: Oxford University Press, 1994, 13-24.

Couteau, Jean, "Preface", *The Sacred Dances of Bali*, Christian Racki, Bali: CV, Buratwangi, 1998.

———, "The Kuta bombing: Wianta's scream of horror", *Made Wianta: Dream Land*, Denpasar: Wianta Foundation, 2003, 36-42.

Covarrubias, Miguel, *The Island of Bali*, Kuala Lumpur: Oxford University Press, 1972.

Crang, Mike, "Cultural Geographies of Tourism", *A Companion to Tourism*, eds., Alan A. Lew, C. Michael Hall, and Alan M. Williams. USA: Blackwell Publishing, 2004. 74-83.

Crick, Malcolm, "Representations of International Tourism in the Social Sciences: Sun, Sex, Sights, Savings, and Servility", *Annual Review of Anthropology*, 18 (1989): 307-44.

Crouch, David, "Tourist Practices and Performances", *A Companion to Tourism*, eds., Alan A. Lew, C. Michael Hall, and Alan M. Williams, USA: Blackwell Publishing, 2004, 85-95.

d' Hauteserre, Anne-Marie, "Postcolonialism, Colonialism and Tourism", *A Companion to Tourism*, eds, Alan A. Lew, C. Michael Hall, and Alan M. Williams, USA: Blackwell Publishing, 2004, 237-45.

Daugherty, Diane, "Fifty Years On: Arts Funding in Kerala Today", *Asian Theatre Journal* 17.2 (Fall 2000): 237-52.

Denzin, Norman K., *Interpretative Ethnography*, London: Sage, 1997.

Dibia, Wayan I., and Rucina Ballinger, *Balinese Dance, Drama and Music*, Singapore: Periplus, 2004.

Dibia, Wayan I., *Kecak: The Vocal Chant of Bali*, Bali: Hartanto Art Books Studio, 2000.

Dunbar-Hall, P., "Tradisi and Tourisme: Music, Dance, and Cultural Transformation at the Ubud Palace, Bali, Indonesia", *Australian Geographical Studies* 41 (1) 2003: 3-16.

Dunbar-Hall, Peter, "Culture, Tourism and Cultural Tourism: boundaries and frontiers in performances of Balinese Music and Dance", *Journal of Intercultural Studies* 22, 2, 2001, 173-87.

Dwikora, Putu Wirata, "Bali and Rites of Bravery", *Made Wianta : Dream Land*, Denpasar: Wianta Foundation, 2003, 43-52.

Eiseman, Fred B. Jr., *Bali : Sekala and Niskala*, vol. I, Berkeley: Periplus, 1996.

Elegantr, R., 1987, "Seeking the Spirits of Bali: Despite Fast Food and Discos, the Old Ways Live", *The New York Times*, 8 March, Section Travel, pp. 9, 26.

Erdman, Joan L., "Dance Discourses: Rethinking the History of the "Oriental Dance", *Moving Words : Re-writing Dance*, ed. Gay Morris, London: Routledge, 1996, 288-305.

Fischer, Michael M.J., "Ethnicity and the Post-modern Arts of Memory", *The Poetics and Politics of Ethnography*, Berkeley; University of California Press: 1986.

Fisk, Josiah, "Classical Music and the Tourist Factor", *The Hudson Review 51*, 150th Anniversary Issue (Spring, 1998): 206-12.

Geertz, Clifford, "Culture and Social Change: The Indonesian Case", *Man, New Series*, vol. 19, no. 4 (December 1984): 511-32.

———, "Form and Variation in Balinese Village Structure", *American Anthropologist*, New Series, vol. 61, no. 6 (December 1959): 991-1012.

———, *Local Knowledge*, New York: Basic Books, 1983.

———, *Negara: The Theatre State in Nineteenth-Century Bali*, USA: Princeton University Press, 1980.

Geertz, H. "Preface", *Mask of Bali*, Judy Slattum, San Francisco: Chronicles Book, 1992.

Godard, Colette, "Shakespeare's Samurai", *Collaborative Theatre*, tr. Eric Prenowitz, David Williams, ed. David Williams, London: Routledge, 1999.

Gorer, Geoffrey, *Bali and Angkor: A 1930s Pleasure Trip Looking at Life and Death*, Singapore: Oxford University Press, 1991.

Herbest, Edward, *Voices in Bali*, Hanover: Wesleyan University Press, 1997.

Hinch, Tom D., "Indigenous People and Tourism", *A Companion to Tourism*, eds., Alan A. Lew, C. Michael Hall, and Alan M. Williams. USA: Blackwell Publishing, 2004, 246-57.

Hough, Brett, "Education for the Performing Arts: Contesting and Mediating Identity in Contemporary Bali", *Staying Local in the Global Village*, eds., Rubinstein and Connor, Honolulu : University of Hawai'i Press, 1999, 231-63.

Howe, Leo, *Hinduism and Hierarchy in Bali*, Great Britain: James Currey, 2001.

Huntington, Samuel P., *The Clash of Civilizations and the Remaking of World Order*, New York: A Touchstone Book, 1996.

Jameson, Fredric, "Postmodernism, or Logic of Late Capitalism", Cultural Sociology, ed. Lyn Spillman, USA: Blackwell, 2002, 341-49.

Jensen, Gordon D., and Luh Ketut Suryani, *The Balinese People: A Reinvention of Character*, New York: Oxford University Press, 1992.

Karnad, Girish, *Three Plays*, New Delhi: OUP, 2000.

Kothari, Sunil and Goverdhan Panchal, "The Rising Importance of Indigenous Theatre in India", *Asian Theatre Journal* 1 (Spring, 1984): 112-14.

Lysloff, Rene T., "Afterword", *Voices in Bali*, Edward Herbest, Hanover: Wesleyan University Press, 1997, 163-69.

MacRae, Graeme, "Acting Global, Thinking Local in a Balinese Tourist Town", *Staying Local in the Global Village*, eds. Rubinstein and Connor, Honolulu: University of Hawai'i Press, 1999, 123-54.

McCarthy, John, *Are Sweet Dreams Made of This*? Australia: Indonesia Resources and Information, 1994.

McPhee, Colin, "Dance in Bali", *Traditional Balinese Culture*, ed. Jane Bello, New York: Columbia University Press, 1970, 290-321.

———, *A House in Bali*, Singapore: Periplus, 2002.

Mead, Margaret, "Children and Ritual in Bali", *Traditional Balinese Culture*, ed. Jane Bello, New York: Columbia University Press, 1970, 198-211.

———, "The Arts in Bali", *Traditional Balinese Culture*, ed. Bello, Jane, New York: Columbia University Press, 1970, 331-40.

———, "The Strolling Players in the Mountains of Bali", *Traditional Balinese Culture*, ed. Jane Bello, New York: Columbia University Press, 1970, 135-45.

———, "Community Drama, Bali and America", *Traditional Balinese Culture*. ed. Jane Bello, New York: Columbia University Press, 1970, 341-49.

Meduri, Avanthi, "Temple Stage as Historical Allegory in Bharatanatyam: Rukmini Devi as Dancer-historian", eds. Indira Viswanathan Peterson and Davesh Soneji, *Performing Pasts: Reinventing the Arts in Modern South India*, New Delhi: Oxford, 2008, 133-64.

Miettinen Jukka O., *Classical Dance and Theatre in South-East Asia*, Oxford University Press: New York, 1992.

Murdoch, James, "Little Known Ubud", *Ubud is a Mood*, Directed and designed by Leonard Lueras, Bali: The Bali Purnati Book, 2004. 102-20.

———, "Introduction", *A House in Bali*, Colin McPhee, Singapore: Periplus, 2002, 5-10.

Ohnuki-Tierney, Emiko, "Introduction", ed. *Culture Through Time*, California: Stanford University Press, 1990.

Panigrahi, Sanjukta, "Five Meetings", *The Performers' Village*, ed. Kirsten Hastrup, tr. Judith Barba and Leo Sykes, Denmark: Drama Nygade, 1996, 88-90.

Pavis, Patrice, ed. "Introduction", *The Intercultural Performance Reader*, London: Routledge, 1996.

Picard, Michael, "Cultural Tourism" in Bali: Cultural Performances as Tourist Attraction", *Indonesia* 49 (April 1990): 37-74.

———, "The Discourse of Kabalian: Transcultural Constructions of Balinese Identity", *Staying Local in the Global Village*, eds. Rubinstein, Raechelle and Connor, Honolulu : University of Hawai'i Press, 1999, 15-49.

———, *Bali: Cultural Tourism and Touristic Culture*, tr. Diana Darling. Singapore: Archipelago Press, 1996.

Pieper, Jan., ed. "An outline of architectural anthropology in relation to the general history and theory of architecture", *Ritual Space in*

India: Studies in Architecture Anthropology, London: Art and Archaeology Research Papers, 1980.

Pitana, I. Gede, "Sociology of Temples: Issues Related to Rivalry in Status and Power", *Bali Living in two Worlds,* tr. I. Gusti Raka Panji Tisna, eds., Urs Ramseyer and I. Gusti Raka Panji Tisna, Schwabe: Museum der Kulturen, 2001, 117-27.

Powell, Hickman, *The Last Paradise,* Singapore: Oxford University Press, 1989.

Preston-Whyte, Robert, "The Beach as a Liminal Space", *A Companion to Tourism,* eds. Alan A. Lew, C. Michael Hall, and Alan M. Williams, USA: Blackwell Publishing, 2004, 349-59.

Putu Wirata Dwikora, "Balinese Society and Contemporary Arts", *Bali Living in Two Worlds,* tr. I. Gusti Raka Panji Tisna, eds. Urs Ramseyer and I Gusti Raka Panji Tisna, Schwabe: Museum der Kulturen, 2001, 143-52.

Racki, Christian, *The Sacred Dances of Bali,* Bali: CV. Buratwangi, 1998.

Ramseyer, Urs, "Bali after the bomb: the dream of a different paradise", *Made Wianta : Dream Land,* Denpasar: Wianta Foundation, 2003, 56-60.

Rana, Jagadish, *Nachganko Raajdhani Bhaktapur,* Kathmandu: Amar Shumsher, 1989.

Reisner, Stefan, "'Foreign' Ubud", *Ubud is a Mood,* Directed and designed by Leonard Lueras. Bali: The Bali Purnati Book, 2004, 138-56.

Robinson, Geoffrey. *The Dark Side of Paradise,* Ithaca: Cornell University Press, 1998.

Roosevelt, Andre, "Introduction", *The Last Paradise,* Hickman Powell, Singapore: Oxford University Press, 1989.

Rosaldo, Renato, "From the Door of His Tent", *The Poetics and Politics of Ethnography,* eds. James and Marcus, Berkeley: University of California Press, 1986, 77-97.

Rubinstein, Raechelle and Linda H. Connor, "Introduction", *Staying Local in the Global Village,* eds. Rubinstein and Connor, Honolulu: University of Hawai'i Press, 1999, 1-14.

Saarinen, Jarkko, "Tourism and Touristic Representations of Nature", *A*

Companion to Tourism, eds., Alan A. Lew, C. Michael Hall, and Alan M. Williams, USA: Blackwell Publishing, 2004, 438-49.

Schechner, Richard and Willa Appel, "Introduction", *By Means of Performance*, New York: Cambridge University Press, 1997, 1-7.

———, *Performative Circumstances From The Avant Garde to Ramlila*, Kolkata: Seagull Books, 1983.

———, "Intercultural Themes", *Performing Arts Journal* 33/34 (XI.3, XII.1):151-62.

Schwartz, Susan L., *Rasa: Performing the Divine in India*, Delhi: Motilal, 2004.

Setia, Putu, "Kuta Encounters", *Traveling to Bali: Four Hundred Years of Journeys*, ed. Adrian Vickers, Kuala Lumpur: Oxford University Press, 1994, 71-77.

Sharma, Chakradhar, "Mantabya." *Kranti ek dishabodh*, Lalitpur: Nepal Prakashan, NS 1125.

Shaw, Gareth, "Entrepreneurial Cultures and Small Business Enterprises in Tourism", *A Companion to Tourism*, eds., Alan A. Lew, C. Michael Hall, and Alan M. Williams, USA: Blackwell Publishing, 2004, 122-33.

Slattum, Judy, *Mask of Bali*, San Francisco: Chronicles Books, 1992.

Slusser, Mary Shepherd, *Nepal Mandala*, Kathmandu: Mandala Book Point, 1998.

Slyomovics, Susan, "Cross-Cultural Dress and Tourist Performance in Egypt", *Performing Arts Journal* 33/34 (vol. XI, no. 3/ vol. XII, no.1): 139-49.

Sorell, Walter, *The Dance through the Ages*, New York: Grosset and Dunlap, 1967.

Sreekumar, T.T. and Govinda Parayil, "Contentions and Contradictions of Tourism as Development Option: The Case of Kerala, India", *Third World Quarterly* 23, 3 (June 2002): 529-548.

Suartaya, Kadek, "Nadi or Kerauhan to Highlight the Performance", *Mudra, Special Edition* (2004) 41-47, Denpasar: Indonesian Institute of the Arts (ISI), 2004.

Subedi, Abhi, *Nepali Theatre as I See It*, Kathmandu: Arohan Gurukul School of Theatre, 2006.

Tenzer, Michael, *Balinese Music*, Singapore: Periplus, 1991.

Throsby, David, "The Production and Consumption of the Arts: A View of Cultural Economics", *Journal of Economic Literature*, vol. 32, no. 1. (March 1994): 1-29.

Tisna, IGR Panji, "The Loss of the Last Paradise?", *Bali Living in two Worlds*, tr. I. Gusti Raka Panji Tisna, eds., Urs Ramseyer and I. Gusti Raka Panji Tisna, Schwabe: Museum der Kulturen, 2001, 15-26.

Tiwari, Sudarshan Raj, *The Brick and Bull: An Account of Handigaun, the Ancient Capital of Nepal*, Kathmandu: Himal Books, 2002.

Turner, Victor, *From Ritual to Theatre*, New York: Paj Publications, 1982.

Urry, John, *The Tourist Gaze*, London: Sage Publications, 2002.

Valeri, Valerio, "Constitutive History: Genealogy and Narrative in the Legitimation of Hawai'ian Kingship", *Culture through Time*, ed. Emiko Ohnuki-Tierney, California: Stanford University Press, 1990, pp. 154-92.

van Ness, Edward C. and Shita Prawirohardjo, *Javanese Wayang Kulit*, New York: Oxford University Press, 1985.

Vatsyayan, Kapila, *Indian Classical Dance*, New Delhi: Ministry of Information and Broadcasting, 1997.

Vickers, Adrian, "Introduction", *Traveling to Bali: Four Hundred Years of Journeys*, ed. Vickers, Kuala Lumpur: Oxford University Press, 1994, xiii-xvi.

———, *Bali: A Paradise Created*, Berkeley: Periplus, 1989.

Wartofsky, Marx W., "Art, Artworlds, and Ideology", *The Journal of Aesthetics and Art Criticism*, vol. 38, no. 3 (Spring, 1980): 239-47.

Wheatley, Bruce P., *The Sacred Monkeys of Bali*, Illinois: Waveland Press, 1999.

Wianta, Made I., "Urs Ramseyer in conversation with Made Wianta", *Made Wianta : Dream Land*, Denpasar: Wianta Foundation, 2003, 61-62.

Wiener, Margaret J., "Making Local History in New Order Bali: Public Culture and the Politics of the Past", *Staying Local in the Global Village*, eds. Rubinstein, Raechelle and Connor, Honolulu: University of Hawai'i Press, 1999, 51-89.

Worsley, Shala, *Categories of Sacred and Non-Sacred in Bali: The People and Notions that Create Them*, Bali: SIT, 1995.

Yarrow, Ralph, *Indian Theatre*, Great Britain: Curzon, 2001.

Zobel, Myron, "An Inn in Klungkung", ed. Adrian Vickers, *Traveling to Bali: Four Hundred Years of Journeys*, Kuala Lumpur: Oxford University Press, 1994, 191-99.

Zoete, Beryl, and Walter Spies, "Dance and Drama in Bali", *Traditional Balinese Culture*, ed. Jane Bello, New York: Columbia University Press, 1970.

Zoete, Beryl and Walter Spies, *Dance and Drama in Bali*, Singapore: Oxford University Press, 1986.

Index